Trails &
Tribes
In Southern Africa

BOOKS BY THE SAME AUTHOR

SANDY TRACKS TO THE KRAALS

THE PEOPLES OF SOUTH AFRICA (3 Volumes)

PATH OF BLOOD—The Rise and Conquests of Mzilikazi,
            Founder of the Matabele

RULE OF FEAR—The Life and Times of Dingane,
            King of the Zulu

HILL OF DESTINY—The Life and Times of Moshesh,
            Founder of the Basotho

PEOPLES OF SOUTHERN AFRICA

TRIBE TO TOWNSHIP

MAURITIUS '62

Peter Becker

Trails & Tribes
In Southern Africa

Photographs by the Author

Hart-Davis, MacGibbon   London

Granada Publishing Limited
First published in Great Britain 1975 by Hart-Davis, MacGibbon Ltd
Frogmore, St Albans, Hertfordshire AL2 2NF and
3 Upper James Street, London W1R 4BP

ISBN 0 246 10768 5
Printed in Great Britain by
William Clowes & Sons, Limited
London, Beccles and Colchester

To
the memory of
MARK LONGMAN

There are times in a man's life when he is humbled by ancient custom, and is made to realize that without an Omnipotent Presence behind the scheme of nature, there would be no source of supply. No life, no growth, no procreation.

From
TRAILS AND TRIBES IN SOUTHERN AFRICA

Contents

Maps

Preface

During twenty years of field research in Southern Africa, I have covered some seventy thousand miles along trails of almost every description. In desert regions to the west they have invariably been no better than the beds of extinct rivers, or game paths or self-made tracks either traced by truck across the dunes, or carved through scrub and thornbush. Trails in the eastern regions have been of a different kind—tortuous, muddy roads, stone-strewn mountain passes, and, in the swampy areas, narrow passages through reed and sedge. All trails have led to the indigenous peoples of Southern Africa, revealing new horizons, new situations and always a host of new and engaging experiences. Never easy to travel, these trails have nonetheless brought untold happiness and constant excitement to my journey through life.

In *Trails and Tribes in Southern Africa* I have been able to do no more than convey my readers to a few of the places, peoples and persons I have visited along the trails. For example, I have made only scant reference to the tribes inhabiting central Southern Africa, some of whom rank among the most colourful I have come to know. In a book to follow I shall deal with this part of the tribal spectrum, with special reference to the way of life, the history and the idiosyncrasies of the peoples of Rhodesia and the South African interior. There is much to be told and to be enjoyed in telling.

On my travels, I have met and befriended many hundreds of people, black, white and brown, to whom I am deeply indebted for the inner wealth I have accumulated. The pages of this book serve both as testimony to the kindnesses, hospitality, help and encouragement I have always received, and as an expression of gratitude to all whose names they bear.

Special thanks, however, are due to D'Arcy Henry of Palapye and Pollie Pollard of Oranjemund for the experiences I shared with them in the Kalahari and Namib Deserts. It is also with profound appreciation that I place on record the names of those African dignitaries whose unflagging cooperation I have enjoyed over the years: the late King Nyangayezizwe Cyprian Bhekuzulu, Chief Gatsha Buthelezi, King Zwelithini KaBhekuzulu, Princess Magogo uZulu KaDinuzulu, Prince Clement Zulu, Mr Walter Kanye, Prince Matthews Zulu, Sir Seretse Khama, King Sobhuza II, Queen Mother Nukwase Nxumalo (deceased), Prince Makhungu Dlamini, Chief Mandanda Mthethwa, Paramount Chiefs Bathoen II, CBE, Kgari Sechele II, OBE (deceased), Archie Velile Sandile (deceased) and Sabata Jonguhlanga Dalindyebo, Chief Ashipala Ipinge, Victor Hugo 'Amigo' Makumbuyo and the late Khotso Sethuntsa.

My thanks are also due to the many government officials for advice and assistance received whilst researching in areas under their jurisdiction.

Finally a special 'thank you' to Connie, Harold, Peter, Nandi, Lindi and Makoti who know the art of treading lightly when there is writing to be done at KwaVulindlela, and to Penny Walley of Mtubatuba for typing my manuscripts.

PETER BECKER
KwaVulindlela
Bryanston
Johannesburg

Introduction

Africa south of the Zambezi River is a land of striking contrasts: in the east it is lush with rolling grassland, bush and forest, and adorned with mountains, streams, lakes and swamps; in the west the earth face is broiled by furnaced skies, fanned by desert winds, threaded with dead or dying rivers, dotted with salt pans and here and there an oasis or subterranean spring. In the central region is an immense plateau—hot in summer, cold in winter and in most parts almost treeless. Southern Africa is a land of uncommon beauty, a vast subcontinent peopled by indigenous desert nomads, swampland dwellers, bushveld cattlemen and tillers and planters scattered over hill, valley and plain.

First contacts between the white and black inhabitants of Southern Africa took place in what is today the Eastern Cape Province, when they came face to face along the Great Fish River in 1770. Some two thousand years before, negro tribes had begun moving slowly southwards from the eastern regions of central Africa, impelled by an ever increasing need for land as their numbers multiplied. Presumably north of the Zambezi River they split into several human streams, meandering into the remotest reaches of the subcontinent: the Nguni, Tsonga and Venda groups into the luxuriant eastern regions; the Ovambo and Herero into the upper limits of South-West Africa, and the large family of Sotho tribes into present-day Botswana, the northern Transvaal and then finally southwards to the banks of the Orange River. And always ahead of them, roaming the interior in hunting bands, were the Khoisan peoples, diminutive, yellow-skinned nomads who, in due course, were to become known colloquially as Bushmen and Hottentots.

The southward expansion of the tribes had petered out by the close of the eighteenth century, and the various Negro groups had settled down to a peaceful, sedentary way of life—tilling and planting, tending their herds and making regular sacrifice to the shades of the dead. This was how the white man found them.

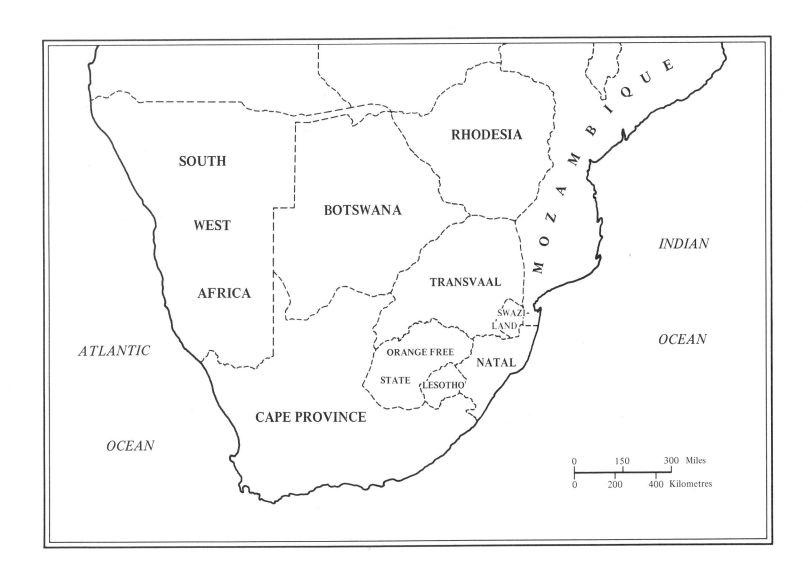

The Bushmen

If one travels today to the Republic of Botswana and especially its Kalahari desert regions, one comes to the Bushmen, in many ways among the most fascinating of all the inhabitants of Southern Africa. Short in stature and lighter by far than the neighbouring black- and brown-skinned African tribes, they are distinctive in appearance, except, of course, in areas where they have interbred with other races. The true Bushman face is spade-shaped and flat, the cranium narrow and the forehead and cheekbones high and prominent. In addition the lower jaw is well-defined, the nose broad and soft, the ears small and lobeless, the scalp sparsely layered with frizzy tufts and the buttocks enormous and flabby, especially among the womenfolk.

The Republic of Botswana mothers some thirty thousand Bushmen scattered over the desert in tiny groups. Over the centuries, as a result of their isolation, most of them have remained untouched by the white man's way of life. To this day, therefore, not only their language, but also their customs and beliefs, reach back into antiquity.

Bushman patriarch of the North-western Kalahari desert, oldest member of a hunting band.

Left Ostrich eggshells in which the nomadic Bushmen store and carry their water.

Below left A Bush woman of the Kalahari desert. Much of her time is devoted daily to collecting edible roots, bulbs, berries and insects in the desert.

Below right The quiver tree (*Acacia Giraffae*) abounds in the western deserts of Southern Africa. Bushmen make quivers from its root-bark.

The Balala

In the course of many years devoted to anthropological research in the Kalahari Desert and South-West Africa, I have found the Bushmen a delightful people, always gentle, always a little shy and reserved at the beginning, but eventually friendly and exceedingly hospitable. West of the huge African settlement of Molepolole, capital of the Bakwena or Crocodile People of Botswana, there is a desolate area called Khudumelapswe, the Place of Tortoises. This part of the desert is inhabited not only by the Crocodile People, but also by their erstwhile serfs, the Bakgalagadi or Kalahari People, as well as a handful of wandering Bushmen called the Balala.

It is no easy matter locating the nomadic Balala in the vastness of the Place of Tortoises. Indeed, were it not for the help of the Crocodile and other Kalahari tribesmen endowed with an uncanny gift for sensing the Bushmen's whereabouts, one might rove the desert, day after day, without success.

The Balala are in the main a hybrid people, having intermarried in generations past with the taller, dark-skinned African tribesmen whose domain they share. In spite of this, they continue to talk a Bushman dialect, and most of their customs and beliefs have remained unchanged.

Balala bands vary in size according to the food potential of the area. So in the climatically unfriendly Place of Tortoises some are no larger than the family unit—a man, his wife and children. The Balala hut, among the simplest human dwellings known to man, is made of a flimsy framework of thornbush branch, crudely covered with grass and scrub. It has no windows, and its doorless entrance is high and wide.

Like other Bush people, past and present, the Balala are hunters of game and collectors of a large variety of edible foods that grow in the desert sands. Their skill in tracking, stalking and snaring is without parallel outside the Kalahari. Their weapons consist of light metal- or bone-tipped arrows which they fire at close range with a short but sturdy bow, a tiny spear, a hunting club, and not infrequently a battered muzzle-loader, presumably procured long ago from white men, and handed down from father to son.

Mindful of the limitations of their weapons, especially when in pursuit of the eland or other of the larger antelopes, the Balala daub their arrows with poisons extracted either from selected

A Balala family of the Lwalle area, Botswana. Balala huts are more sturdily built than those of Bushmen in more westerly regions.

roots, bark and berries, or from the venom sacs of snakes, spiders or scorpions. Poisons are also prepared from the cocoons and grubs of a reddish-brown desert beetle, and even from stones. These vary from band to band, depending upon what is available in the immediate environment.

During a hunt the Balala move cautiously into action, first stalking their quarry like a genet or field rat, and then attacking with a melodic 'ping' of their bows. An unsuspecting springbok, suddenly startled by the pang of an arrow imbedded in its side, flashes away followed in its tracks by a pair of fleetfooted Balala huntsmen. Soon it falters, the poison ebbing away its strength, and then it staggers and falls on its nose into the sands. The Balala pounce swiftly, and stab it to death with spears. Then after a short rest they head for home carrying the carcass between them.

Meanwhile the Balala womenfolk have been ranging the vicinity of the huts in search of veldfoods, returning at midday with a good supply of edible roots, bulbs, tubers, fruits, seeds and berries. Some are bound to have collected thirst-quenching succulents, some a number of juicy desert watermelons known as the *tsamma*, and others bowls of wild cucumber. And the children? They have been noisily scrambling for grasshoppers, locusts, flying ants, crickets, grubs and lizards. One of the youths might even have killed a puff-adder to be roasted for the evening meal.

When night falls over the Place of Tortoises, fires come to life at the Balala encampments. Looking back some fifteen years, I can see myself seated beside one of these fires in the company of fourteen Balala. My nostrils, I recall, had relished the inviting aroma of roasting springbok, adder, insects and grass seeds. But when the time arrived for eating, I nibbled fastidiously at the bits of flesh I was obliged to share with my over-generous hosts. The feasting continued throughout the night amidst ceaseless chattering, spasmodic belching and occasional yawning. Catching sight of the rising morning star, my eyes leaden with want of sleep, my lungs smarting with logfire smoke, I withdrew eventually from the little circle of friends, and slid into my sleeping bag. There was nothing as fatiguing, I told myself, floating away into the shadows of sleep, as a Bushman feast that follows the hunt. Nothing.

Balala family taking refuge beneath the thorn-trees from the onslaught of the desert midday sun.

Endemic Syphilis

Some of the happiest and unhappiest moments of my life have been spent in the company of Balala Bushmen. In contrast to the many delightful times I have spent among them at the Place of Tortoises, I recall the anguish I was to suffer in 1958 when, as a member of Dr Rudolph Bigalke's Alexander McGregor Museum expedition, I came into contact with an impoverished Balala encampment in the Maokane district, south of the desert track that leads to Ghansi.

We had located the Balala on the morning of 10 September. The band had numbered no more than six adults and eleven children, all housed in three rickety huts. About a hundred paces from the little encampment was a fourth hut, which I noticed was not only smaller than the others but also far more flimsy. I remember wondering why it had been built in isolation from the others, and deciding to investigate at my first opportunity.

No sooner had we exchanged greetings with the little band, than we realized all its members were infected with *tholosa* or endemic syphilis, the most dreaded scourge of the desert. Moreover, all the children had *dikgwaba* in various stages, an unsightly favus infection of the scalp resembling a layer of dried-out honeycomb. Both *tholosa* and *dikgwaba* had become part of the lives of this Bushman band, and a source of attraction to myriad flies that thronged their spongy scalps, watery eyes, runny noses and, indeed, every face, chest and limb blemished with syphilitic lesions.

There was a middle-aged man with bulbous eyes, a festering hole where his nose had been, and his private parts, the little that remained of them in the wake of the *tholosa*, heavily ulcerated. His wife was also covered with sores, her nose a hollow scab, and the nipples of her meagre breasts—she was feeding a six-month-old baby at the time—inflamed with infection. The faces and chests of the children were dotted with white-headed, wart-like eruptions, and their tongues, lips and throats coated with florid, mucous patches. Finally, the worst of all, there was the 'human animal', as the Balala called him, an elderly patriarch whom we found in the isolated hut outside the encampment. Coming face to face with this man was a saddening experience, one I strive in vain to forget.

He was curled up on the floor of the little grass hut, all but his feet covered by a jackal-skin kaross. Hearing me greet him, he rose slowly on to an elbow, drew aside the kaross, and exposed a faceless head. Nose, lips and cheeks had been eaten away by *tholosa*! And, as he struggled to speak, flies fussed about him, crowding his jawbones and making excursions into his mouth. I was amazed that one so mutilated, so feeble and so very

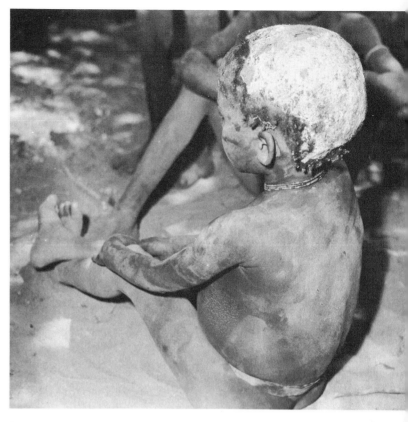

A Balala child, its scalp covered with *dikgwaba*, a favus infection.

distressed could muster the strength to respond to my call.

We remained with the stricken old man for no longer than a minute or two, and returning to the encampment found that the Balala had formed themselves into little groups, adults and children apart, and were seated side by side in the ash-strewn sand near the huts. The syphilitic woman was no longer feeding her baby, but with the aid of a sharpened stick was opening the fungous sores on its scalp. Close by a greybeard, bald from the ravages of *dikgwaba* in days gone by, was letting blood from the middle-aged man with the bulbous eyes. An extraordinary sight: an example of Bushman surgery reminiscent of medieval times. Having made deep incisions on the patient's cheeks, a little below the eyes, the greybeard cupped first the left one and then the right with an antelope horn opened at the tip and sucked. His intention was not only to relieve his friend's body of impure blood, but also his soul of the evil influence behind the hideous *tholosa* disease. The bleeding over, flies swarmed in to feed.

Towards the end of the following year, almost fifteen months after our meeting with the syphilitic Balala, I was researching

A young Bushman of the Rakopo area. Infected with *tholosa* or endemic syphilis, he might have died had he not been located and treated by the World Health Organization.

again in the Kalahari Desert, but on this occasion among the Balala of the Lwalle district. One morning, curious to know how our stricken friends of Maokane were faring, I arranged for a guide to take me there. We located the little band not far from where Bigalke and I had found them in 1958, and I was delighted to observe they had been cured of both *tholosa* and *dikgwaba*. They looked almost radiant with health. On enquiry I was told they had been visited and given treatment by members of the World Health Organization, and, like thousands of Bush and Tswana victims before them, had been 'miraculously' restored to health.

And what of the faceless one, I asked, whom we had seen in the isolated hut? He was no longer with them, replied the Balala, having passed away two months before. He had died willingly, knowing he had long been victim to a sorcerer's curse, and was doomed to succumb to *tholosa*. Nothing could save him. Least of all the medicines those kindly white men had brought.

Tswana Tribes

The Republic of Botswana is a vast territory some three quarters of a million square kilometres in area. Stinted by meagre and precarious rains, it is bitten to the core by a vicious sun all the year round, and during wintry nights, by freezing winds. Wedged between South-West Africa on the one side and the South African Republic on the other, it is among the most sparsely populated states of the African continent.

Botswana is divided into eight large tribal areas, each headed by a supreme or paramount chief, and each area in turn subdivided into districts ruled by lesser chiefs, and in some of the remoter parts, by headmen. At the head of the entire Tswana nation is a president, who, together with all other members of his parliament, is voted into office by the general electorate. The

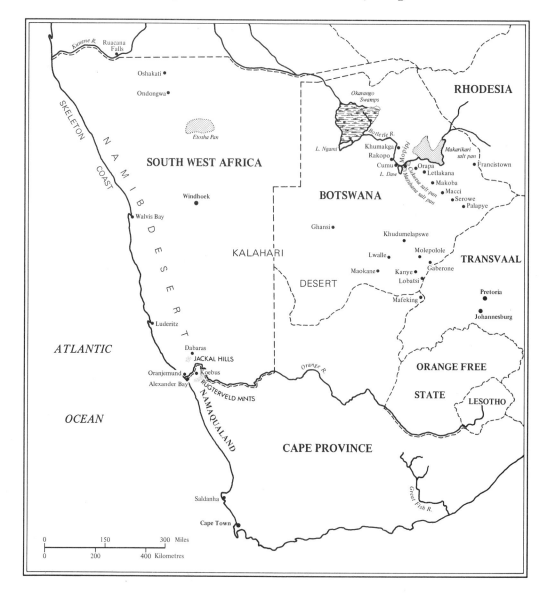

A Tswana *kgotla* or tribal court in session.
Kanye Royal Village, Botswana.

seat of government, once ironically situated in Mafeking, beyond the Botswanan border, was moved at the time of independence to Gaberone, which had long been earmarked as the country's capital.

In comparison with territories to the east Botswana is climatically unfriendly, but this drawback is amply compensated for by its rustic beauty, and above all by the general warmheartedness of its population.

The first Tswana-speaking inhabitants of Botswana were the Bakgalagadi or Kalahari People, vanguard of the great Sotho migration from the north. On arrival in the country they met up with the Bushmen, whom they either dispersed into the desert or enslaved. Then in the seventeenth century, coinciding roughly with the settlement of white men in the Cape Colony, other more powerful Tswana tribes began moving in, elbowing the Kala-

hari people out of the more fertile regions into the desert wastelands. In the territory west of Molepolole the Bakgalagadi were to be decimated by the Crocodile People and reduced to serfdom. Thereafter it was their lot to bring regular tribute to their overlords—pelts, hides, horns and ostrich feathers—in return for periodic gifts of sorghum. Indeed, even to this day the Kalahari People are basically a servile folk, recognizing the Bakwena, Bangwaketsi, Bamangwato and other main Tswana tribes as superiors.

The Tswana live in villages, some of them small, and others with populations exceeding thirty thousand. Kanye, Serowe, Molepolole and Shoshong, to name but a few, comprise a multiplicity of thatched rondavel-style huts (round with conical thatched roofs), grouped in family units and surrounded by *lapas*, high, clay walls. Each settlement has a conspicuous central

Councillors of the *Kgatla* tribe of Botswana
chatting in the shade of a *marulla* tree, in the
kgotla or tribal court of Mosupha royal village.

section occupied by the paramount chief, or, as in the case of less
important villages, by a chief or headman. It is here that the
kgotla or gathering place is situated, a palisade enclosure where
meetings called by the rulers are held, and where transgressors
are brought to trial.

An interesting feature of the Tswana way of life is that the
important villages are seldom fully occupied for longer than the
period from the end of the reaping season in July to the beginning of spring in October. The reason is that in Botswana the
sorghum and maize lands and the melon and groundnut gardens
are scattered over a vast area surrounding the villages, some as

close by as five kilometres and others as far distant as eighty.
Invariably grazing grounds for the hundreds of thousands of
cattle are even farther afield. So usually tribesmen employed in
tilling, planting or herding require at least two homes—one in
the main village for the winter months (July to October), and
another in the vicinity of the lands or a cattlepost for the remainder of the year.

The Tswana are a peace-loving people. In the nineteenth
century they were involved in a number of wars, but these were
mainly in defence of their country against the Matabele armies
of the conqueror Mzilikazi, and the Batlokwa or Wild Cat hordes

Bathoen II, formerly Paramount Chief of the
Bangwaketsi tribe, Botswana.

Old woman of a Kgalagadi clan near Lwalle,
Botswana.

of the fearsome, female marauder, Mantatisi. They have never been a nation of warriors in the mould of the warlike Zulu. In battle, although as adequately armed as the best of their foes, their strategy was often lamentably poor and their defences entirely inadequate.

Often whilst collecting material for my biography of the legendary Mzilikazi, I visited Tswana *kgotlas* or gathering places, sharing discussion with Bakwena and other tribal chroniclers in the shade of a spreading tree. For hours sometimes we would delve into the past, recounting the highlights of Tswana military history. What emerged was not so much the glorious deeds of

national heroes as the magnificent regalia the warriors had worn into battle, the foods they had eaten or could not eat and the weapons they had used.

So one would learn from the chroniclers that the Bamangwato in the north, the most powerful of the Tswana tribes, had been armed with long, double-barbed javelins; assegais both smooth-bladed and barbed and varying in length and weight; serrated arrows fired with sinew-strung bows; battle-axes, and finally, knob-headed combat clubs. The warriors had been proudly attired in distinctive regalia—loin cloths, tippets and feathery headdresses. They made designs on their faces, bodies and limbs with clays of many colours, and they adorned their necks, wrists and ankles with amulets.

And today? The age-old regimental system has long since fallen into disuse, and even in the villages traditional tribal dress has been forsaken in preference for European clothing. Under the energetic influence of the pioneer missionaries Moffat, Livingstone and McKenzie, and others who came after them, the Tswana tribes were quick to adapt to material change. Christianity spread rapidly and throve, albeit not always in an orthodox form. Schools sprang up, and in answer to the demand among the newer generations for enlightenment they have both multiplied and flourished over the years. Hence the emergence of a middle-class élite in villages and towns hugging the railway line from Lobatsi to Francistown, and the growth of small and large-scale businesses owned and controlled by the Tswana themselves.

To the west, however, in the more sparsely populated desert regions, much of the indigenous Tswana culture has remained untouched by Western norms. Indeed, in those far-off parts there are tribes whose way of life is as austere today, as it was in the time preceding the advent of missionary enterprise.

D'Arcy Henry beside the truck used for crossing the desert into North-western Botswana.

The North-Western Trail

Although during the past eighteen years I have returned at regular intervals to Botswana, I count among the most memorable of my trips the one that began on 3 December 1967. It was not the most instructive, nor even the most exciting, but by far the happiest, if only because of the company of my guide, D'Arcy Henry of Palapye, a veteran traveller in the desert.

Tall, lean and as hardy as hippo hide, D'Arcy has criss-crossed the desert for some thirty years, making contact with its peoples and absorbing their customs, beliefs and idiosyncrasies. He is essentially an outdoor man but, like others of his breed whom I have met in the remotest parts of Southern Africa, has read widely and, indeed, is as versed in world affairs as most city-dwellers I know. But D'Arcy is at his best in the desert where he is intimately known and welcomed as a friend by tribesmen and Bushmen alike. There seems to be nothing more pleasing to their ears than the drone of D'Arcy Henry's approaching truck.

Our journey into the interior on that memorable December morning began at Palapye in sluicing rain, a happy omen in a territory endlessly haunted by drought. Our first stop was at Serowe, capital village of the Bamangwato tribe, the birthplace of Botswana's first president, Sir Seretse Khama. There we loaded provisions, topped up the truck's water and petrol tanks, and after lighting our pipes trundled westwards along the nar-

row track that leads to the desert. Soon we passed Serowe's sacred hill, on the crest of which the tribe's royal burial grounds are situated. To the left and right were row upon row of huts and palisaded cattlefolds, and in the road fowls, goats and pigs all scampering to safety at the sight of the truck. The rain had lifted by the time we climbed into the hills beyond the village, to be replaced by swift-gathering mists. Now we struck out for Macci, a cattlepost on the eastern fringe of the desert, suddenly gliding through avenues of yellow-plumed *moralala* trees interspersed with the white-leafed *letajwana*. With us in the truck were two Tswana men, Gonkang and Mangatau, both as conversant with the whims of the desert as D'Arcy Henry himself.

We travelled for almost an hour before reaching Macci. It was a medium-sized Tswana cattlepost fronted by rambling stockades and two tanks on stilts into which water was being pumped from a borehole. Hundreds of cattle flocked around a line of concrete drinking troughs positioned below the tanks. Creeping slowly by, we were besieged by a pack of loop-tailed dogs, all yapping hysterically, and ignoring the friendly greetings we exchanged with their masters, the herdsmen of Macci. The track led into bushy country, and we skirted two more Macci cattleposts similar to the first. By midday we had ploughed through the villages of Kugai and Makoba, and were bound for an oasis called Letlakana.

During the early afternoon the clouds parted and the sun

The eastern corner of Serowe, royal village of Sir Seretse Khama, president of Botswana.

A Hurutsi herdboy and his sisters drawing water from one of the shallow wells at Letlakana.

The track east of Orapa after a thunder storm.

broke through, casting a blinding glare across an immense terrain of soggy, chalky-white sand. Soon afterwards the desert was lost in a blanket of steam, suddenly to appear again, having been quickly restored to its usual crispy dryness by the fierce onslaught of the sun. A few thorntrees bent and battered by years of exposure to desert sandstorms dotted the surroundings. Beneath their scanty shade were clusters of goats, their heads huddled together as they panted in the heat.

Letlakana is known in that part of the desert for its fresh-water pits, flanked on the one side by a large village of the Bahurutsi tribe, and on the other by scrub. On arrival we found some herdboys filling a wooden trough with water drawn from one of the pits. Close by three tribesmen, mounted wide-legged on donkeys, drank leisurely from homemade goatskin water-bags, which presumably they had just filled in preparation for a journey into the desert. A fourth man dressed in shirt, shorts and leggings came striding down to the pits along a goat path, and in due course we all came together at the drinking troughs, exchanging lengthy greetings as is the custom in Tswana territory.

Where did we come from, and what was the purpose of our visit to Letlakana? asked the man with the leggings, introducing himself as Sergeant Koketso Ntshebe of the Botswana police. Had we heard about the murders, six in all, committed in the neighbourhood in recent years? These had been ritual killings, the victims' bodies dismembered and used by medicine men for their magical decoctions. In one case a disembodied head, stripped of eyes, cheeks, ears, nose and tongue, had been found buried in the village *kgotla*. The culprit's intention had been to cast a spell on the chief and councillors, thereby deadening their powers of detection. He and four others had since been arrested, convicted and hanged, and their several accomplices sent to jail to dwell on their sins. While the sergeant spoke I reflected on the prevalence of this heinous practice in Lesotho, Swaziland and other parts of Southern Africa, including urban areas on the outskirts of Johannesburg. It is an ancient practice which demands that the victim be carefully selected for the special qualities he is known to possess—wisdom, farsightedness, and valour, to name but a few.

Taking leave of him with an assurance that we had no intention of remaining in Letlakana, we retraced our steps to the truck and drove away, throwing up clouds of the chalky-white dust.

By evening we had entered the Orapa district where the desert sands are soft and deep, and where *mopani* trees grow in great profusion, their delicate multi-coloured leaves shimmering like fairyland lights in the rays of the setting sun. The desert track meanwhile had become impassable in parts, churned all day into deep slush by lorries that had been travelling to and from the nearby Orapa diamond fields. Detours were difficult to make, for the *mopani* trees were too big and the undergrowth too dense for the customary practice of 'riding the bush'. Despite every precaution our truck whined to a skidding halt, sinking on to its axles in the sodden sands. So we took out spades and dug around the wheels, packing them tightly with *mopani* branches stripped from the trees about us. Then, at a signal from D'Arcy, Gonkang, Mangatau and I, amidst the roar of the engine and the whirling of the rear wheels, pushed from behind. Little by little the truck started shuddering forward, until eventually it squelched its way on to a drier patch in the track ahead. By this time the sun had set, so we veered into a clearing among the *mopani* trees, and pitched camp for the night.

When one travels in the desert nothing is as pleasant as bully-beef stew, served in an enamel plate and washed down with a mug of steaming coffee. And when there is no moon, and the Kalahari sky is a sooty black, the stars throbbing with an uncommon brilliance, there is no place more beautiful to sleep in than a clearing embraced by *mopani* forest.

You awake next morning, your ears filled with bird song, and your nostrils with the sweet aroma of a desert breeze. Then your eyes fall on puddles of moisture entrapped in the hollows and pleats of your canvas counterpane, and you marvel at the weight of the dew. And if you should be travelling with D'Arcy Henry, you break camp early and move on in the cool of the morning. No breakfast. Just a cup of black coffee, and a promise that you will be stopping for a 'bite of brunch', somewhere along the side of the track.

From Orapa the desert trail cuts westwards through the *mopani* for twenty-five kilometres. Then, as it drops gradually into a seemingly boundless valley beyond, it leaves the forest behind.

We moved quickly through the valley, following the edge of the Cukutsa salt pan, where the surface was crunchy and smooth. After Cukutsa, the Matshana pan. It was there that we came upon a flight of mallard and red-billed teal, three of which D'Arcy bagged with a single shot for our evening meal. Leaving the Matshana pan we skirted the shores of Lake Daw, reaching Mopipi just before noon. This was a huge village inhabited mainly by Kalanga, Batete and Damara tribesmen. It overlooked another of the countless salt pans that dot these remote parts of the desert.

Mopipi at midday is no place for white people unaccustomed to the dazzling glare projected by salt-caked soil, or to heat that bites through clothes. After a brief discussion with a local headman in the shade of a leathery-branched *mopipi* tree, we moved on into a wasteland recently blown bare by a succession of sandstorms. On arrival at a small Kalanga village along the way, we

D'Arcy Henry, Gonkang and Mangatau watching for mallard and red-billed teal in the Matshana salt pan.

Kalanga village near the Daukudi drift.

Left Kalanga tribesmen about to cross the Daukidi drift near Lake Daw.

Below left Makoba village with granaries, between Cumu and Rakopo.

Below right Kalanga granaries on the outskirts of Rakopo.

Kalanga cattlepost at Rakopo

stopped to converse with tribesmen mounted on donkeys and armed with patched-up muzzle-loaders. Farther on we came suddenly to the banks of the Botletle river which links both Lake Ngami and the Okavango swamps in the north with Lake Daw in the south. There were scores of Kalanga crossing the river over the shallow, stone-strewn Daukudi drift, the menfolk astride tousle-haired donkeys, and their wives following on foot. In the rapids below the drift, a line of youths were scooping fish from the stream with baskets—copper bream, pike and poison-spiked squeakers. On the opposite bank a drove of cattle came lumbering over the sands to drink at the water's edge. There was not a tree, not a shrub, nor even a boulder in sight. And the heat continued to bite.

We crossed the drift after a hasty 'brunch', and by two o'clock found ourselves threading through a series of villages nestled in a sun-bleached flat called Cumu. We crossed into a grove of giant *mogoto* trees, their twisted branches stripped of leaves by monstrous winds, their roots intertwined on the sands like struggling serpents, their trunks bent to the east.

Beyond Cumu lies Rakopo, a network of Kalanga cattleposts, each comprising a sea of reed-thatch rondavel huts and a string of lofty stockades. On arrival at the settlement we drew up at a solitary trading store on a rise overlooking the settlement. Built wholly of corrugated iron, it creaked and crackled in the sun, its roof sending up shimmering waves of heat. The temperature was intense, not unlike that of a boiler room, the air stagnant and fetid.

From Rakopo we set out for Khumakga which lies sixty kilometres to the north along the upper reaches of the Botletle river. We reached the first of the villages an hour before sunset, our

Members of a Bushman band ten miles south of Rakopo.

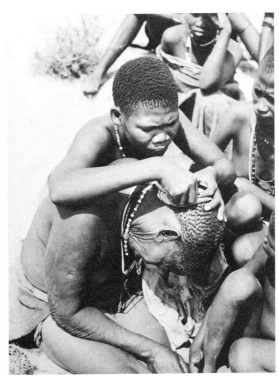

Far left One of the many species of huge edible tubers dug out of the sands by Bushmen and other desert dwellers.

Left Bush children take turns in delousing the elders of the band.

Elderly Bush woman.

Oldest member of a Bushman band located near Rakopo.

eyes smarting, our spines aching and our bodies itching with sweat. Then, quite unexpectedly, came the most rewarding moment of the journey: slithering over a sand dune, we beheld before us the Botletle river, a magnificent expanse of crystal water adorned with lilac-tinted lilies and vast expanses of bulrush and bamboo sedge. A huge flotilla of pelicans sailed past us against the gentle stream, plunging their massive heads into the water in perfect unison, and paying no heed to the cormorants, egrets and spurwing geese that flew this way and that above them.

During the time that remained before nightfall, we quickly pitched camp on the left bank of the river, beneath a canopy of overhanging trees. We then took to the water in a flat-bottomed boat.

The river was clear and cool like a mountain spring. Deep down shoals of bream and yellow fish flicked past us, and in the gathering darkness we could see the shadowy shapes of crocodiles lurking at the edge of the sedges. Along the river's eastern shore, where the soil is black and rich with floodwater sludge, two Kalanga tribesmen, assisted by youths, were ploughing and planting sorghum seed, unconcerned by the fast-fading light. Meanwhile the surroundings had filled with night sounds— the whimpering of jackal, the piping of a fish eagle and the distant grunting of lions. It was almost dark when we returned to the water's edge and then to camp. We had decided to get to bed early. We would be departing in the morning for a Bushman encampment south of Rakopo.

Although one usually sleeps out in the open under the stars when travelling in the desert in summer, on that night at Khumakga we were driven into tents by a bombardment of thunder and lightning, followed by a gentle drizzle. At about three o'clock in the morning we were rocked from our slumbers by the roar of lions and the giggle of hyenas. Sitting erect in our sleeping bags, D'Arcy with a rifle clutched in his hands, we probed the surroundings with our sensitive ears. As is customary at a frightening moment like this, we stacked up the camp fire with logs, lighting the surrounding bush with a comforting glow. But as it seemed that the roars and giggles were growing louder the four of us sat in silence beside the fire, counting the minutes to the first light of dawn. Never have I known the sun to rise so beautifully as on that December morning. Never has a desert sun filled me with so much gladdening warmth.

We broke camp under a cloudless sky and in sweltering heat, loaded the truck, and struck out for Rakopo. Four hours later we located the Bushmen near a salt pan beyond the settlement, a band of thirty-two adults and children of various ages, living in eight little huts.

During the following week whilst I worked among the Rakopo Bushmen in the midst of desolation, I was filled with admiration for their attitude to life in general and to each other in particular. In comparison with the Balala and the other tribes scattered over the wastes of Botswana, the Rakopo Bushmen are uniquely dependent upon the environment, and each other, for survival; and they live in an enviable harmony with nature. I noticed how eager they were to share with each other their meagre possessions, especially tit-bits of food, and how when an elderly woman complained of an aching head they fussed around her pouring out words of solicitude. Nothing seemed to please them more than to eat and chatter together in a small circle by the fireside, and then later to sing, dance and romp together. Small wonder these folk are known to abhor violence, condemn cruelty and discourage dissension. In their very simplicity they reflect the essence of spiritual bigness, providing their visitor with an abundance of proverbial food for thought.

The Hottentots

When the Dutch under Jan van Riebeeck settled in the vicinity of Table Bay in 1652, they soon came into contact with the indigenous inhabitants of the Cape Peninsula—tiny yellow-skinned folk who referred to themselves as Khoi-Khoin, or Men of Men. So amused were the settlers at the so-called 'gibberish' the Khoi-Khoin spoke, that they called them the 'Huttentut', meaning 'the stammerers', a name that was to change with the years into 'Hottentot'. It was at first a friendly meeting, but one fated to bring to a close the carefree existence hitherto pursued by the Men of Men.

Not long after they had established their peninsular settlement, the Dutch also met up with Bushmen, whom they found resembled the Hottentots in many ways. The two peoples were similar in appearance; both hunted game with bows and arrows, ranged the veld in search of edible foods, carried their water in ostrich egg-shells and spoke a peculiar 'click-click' language.

There were also striking differences. Though neither took part in tilling and planting, the Hottentots were breeders of long-horned cattle, fat-tailed sheep and goats, whereas the Bushmen kept no stock at all. Furthermore, Hottentot dwellings, compared with the Bushmen's flimsy shelters, were sturdy, and made rainproof with a thick covering of mats woven from reeds. These dome-shaped huts stood side by side in circular formation, facing inwards on to a yard where the stock was housed after dark. Hottentot kraals were surrounded by thornbush hedges, while those of the Bushmen had no protection against thieves or beasts of prey.

In the decades following van Riebeeck's arrival at the Cape, as the Dutch moved inland to hunt or graze their stock, they came upon Hottentot settlements as far afield as the Orange river in the north, the Kei river in the east and the arid regions beyond Saldanha Bay in the west. They were to learn that these Men of Men consisted of several tribes—the Goringhaikona, Kora, Grigriqua, Inqua, Damaqua, Gonaqua and Nama to name but a few.

Within a year of their first meeting in the peninsula, the Dutch and the Hottentots began squabbling over grazing rights, and became involved in a series of battles leading first to the Hottentots' defeat and dispersal, and in due course to the movement of fugitive hordes towards the north. Many were to be butchered by Xhosa-speaking tribal Africans, and their womenfolk captured and turned into concubines. By the turn of the century a great many of the original Hottentot women, both those who had fled into the interior and those who had remained behind at the Cape, had intermarried with other races—African tribesmen, white settlers and imported Negro slaves. Several hybrid groups emerged, among them the Griqua, Koranna and Orlams.

Throughout the eighteenth century the half-breed Hottentots

grew in power, coming into possession of horses and contraband firearms. They were therefore a constant threat to the white colonial farming community, and subject to unending strife. Eventually, seething with discontent, they began trekking northwards. By 1800 the Griqua, under leadership of Barend Barends, had occupied what is today Griqualand West, where they grazed their cattle and fat-tailed sheep, and hunted antelope in the surrounding veld.

In the meantime the Koranna, headed by Jan Bloem who in years past had attacked and pillaged tribal villages throughout central South Africa, had occupied a strip of territory between the Harts and Vaal rivers, and the Orlams the northern regions of Namaqualand. Because of incessant droughts and the pangs of poverty, large numbers of Griqua and Koranna formed into bands of banditti and embarked on marauding expeditions into the western and eastern tribal areas.

Thus was born a fraternity of desperadoes who were to become known as Bergenaars, or Mountain Men, the most powerful band of horsemen ever to scavenge the Cape, Orange Free State and Caledon flats. They set fire to kraals, villages and missionary settlements, pillaging granaries and butchering tribesmen who dared to cross their paths. Before long, due to the terror they left in their wake, the South African interior swarmed with a rabble of refugees, bound either for the Lesotho highlands or for the bushy regions of Botswana.

The Orlams, although not marauders in the Bergenaar mould, were nevertheless also a belligerent people. Settled temporarily among the Nama Hottentots south of the Orange river, they moved northwards into South-West Africa in the 1830s, and under the leadership of Jonker Afrikander attacked and defeated the Negro Herero tribes in the vicinity of present-day Windhoek.

In the years to follow the Griqua, Koranna, Bergenaars and Orlams might well have entered other parts of Southern Africa had they not been crushed, each in turn, by invading tribal armies: the Griqua and Koranna by the mighty Matabele under the conqueror Mzilikazi; the Bergenaars mainly by the Basotho of Moshesh I and the Orlams by the blood-thirsty Herero. Even the sedentary Nama, joining forces with their Orlams kinsmen, were drawn into the South-West African conflict.

In due course, from the northern Cape to Windhoek the hybrid Hottentots were reduced to impoverishment, and to add to their misery their numbers were depleted severely by a sudden surge of smallpox that swept through their encampments. Today they are a gentle and peace-loving people, friendly, hospitable and bubbling with an enormous facility for humour. By far the majority have lost their colourful 'click-click' language, speaking instead a brand of Afrikaans tinctured with indigenous idiom. Only in areas remote from white and tribal Southern Africa are traces of their former dialects and culture still to be found. It was with this thought in mind that I set out for Koebus in 1971, a district in the southern reaches of South-West Africa's Namib Desert, inhabited by descendants of the Nama people.

The Nama

Koebus lies to the east of Alexander Bay and Oranjemund, the diamond towns lipping the mouth of the Orange river. I arrived

Namaqualand farm.

in Oranjemund in June and was shown to the office of Boeps Wessels, a personnel manager on the diamond fields, and in former times a tribal commissioner stationed in the heart of the Koakaveld. Having learned some weeks before of my intention to visit the Nama, Wessels had already opened the way for my visit to Koebus. The mine owned a farm called Beauvallon on the banks of the river. I would be taken next morning to meet its manager, Pollie Pollard, who for some twenty years had made regular trips to Koebus. Pollard was a product of Namaqualand and, apart from his intimate knowledge of Nama custom, he knew the ecology of the Namib desert.

The farm, Beauvallon, adorns the southern bank of the Orange river like a mammoth emerald set in the tortured dunes of the surrounding desert. Driven to the homestead by jeep at dawn, I found Pollard waiting for me at the kitchen door. He was a squat, barrel-chested man of fifty-five, his face tawny and cragged like a weathered sandstone krantz, and his rolled-up shirt sleeves revealing powerful arms.

Over a cup of coffee we discussed his lifelong friendship with the Nama and other Hottentot peoples of Namaqualand and South-West Africa. He assured me I would enjoy my visit to Koebus. However, before I made contact with the Nama he would take me into the Namib desert and show me some of its scenic wonders. This would help me equate the Nama mind with the humble Nama way of life.

The northern bank of the Orange river, overlooking Beauvallon, rises from the water's edge in a succession of elongated folds. Worn smooth by the wind, it has come to resemble a gigantic colon, hence its name, Grootderm. Above the 'colon',

crowning a ridge of dunes, looms a fort, used by the Germans before the First World War as a police post. It was now in ruins and said to be prowled after dark by the ghost of a Nama maiden. An eroded track pencilled into the folds of Grootderm by camel patrols stood out white like a bloodless vein. On that morning in June, as we watched the red of the rising sun creep over the desert and into the river, Grootderm seemed suddenly to twist and turn and swell with life.

Dabaras

Pollie Pollard and I set out for the desert by truck soon after sunrise. The road from Beauvallon farm climbs, drops and winds in and out of saddles of rock along the course of the river. It threads through a table-top flat of ash-grey scrub, past a Namaqualand shepherd's solitary, whitewashed shack and across a tumble-down village once inhabited by labourers employed on the Alexander Bay diamond fields. Crossing the Orange river we cut through rolling beige-coloured dunes, following a track made by vehicles from the mine. A line of telephone poles to the left of us was almost buried in the shifting sands. In fact, in parts the dunes had crept as high as the overhead wires.

'When the sandstorms blow,' said Pollard, 'the landscape can change overnight. The dunes start moving from place to place, burying buildings, cars and trees and forcing even the river to change its course.'

Ten kilometres farther on the sands came abruptly to an end, and we entered a vast undulation of stony terrain and scattered

Shepherd's home, Namaqualand.

Hottentot grave in the Namib desert.

'Hottentot's candle' plant.

scrub. Jerking to a halt, Pollard jumped from the truck, and beckoning me to follow he climbed up a little rise, where two piles of stone lay side by side.

'Graves,' he said. 'Transport riders from the north who used to bring provisions for the Germans stationed at the fort, and fodder for the camels. They met their death right here, nobody knows how, and then their donkeys broke loose from the wagon and started roaming the desert in search of water. So today not only do we have gemsbok in these parts, but also a large number of tattered, long-eared donkeys as wild and cunning as our jackals.'

I shall always look back on those two lone graves as the spot where my introduction to Namib plant life began. During the following two hours we criss-crossed that section of the desert, Pollard the teacher and I as keen a student as he is ever likely to meet.

In all my years of field research, I have marvelled at the attunement of our indigenous peoples to the environment that serves their needs. Most fascinating of all has been the study of the ecology in the arid, western regions, as compared with that of the luxuriant east. I have always found it a sobering thought, however, that although deserts I have visited abound with nature's food in no less a measure than parts of water-logged Mozambique, year after year white travellers lost in the Kala-

hari have died of hunger and thirst, often within arm's length of edible and thirst-quenching roots and berries.

The first Namib plant shown me by Pollard was a desert creeper known to Nama Hottentots as the *cwibi*.

'They say it has magical qualities,' he said, 'because should you be thirsty, and I mean really thirsty, all you need do is chew a piece of its root, and within minutes you'll be rid of the craving.'

We moved on from plant to plant, from the widely spread inedible ashbush scrub to a waxy-stemmed xerophyte, which when lit burns brightly, and is known as the 'Hottentot's Candle'. We also saw the white-flowered *brakslaai*, a hairy long-fingered succulent used by the Nama for removing the fur from pelts.

'They make a mash of the leaves,' Pollard explained, 'kneading it well into the fur, and then covering the whole with sand. Next day they shake out the skin, and not only does the mash come away, but also the fur. Where there are Nama settlements like the one at Koebus, *brakslaai* is in constant demand.'

A striking phenomenon of this part of the Namib Desert is the abundance of vegetation that sprouts from out of its seemingly lifeless surface after as little as half a centimetre of rain. Strewn with seed carried by the winds from the Namaqualand flats, beyond the Orange river, it becomes suddenly carpeted with mauve calendula and Namaqualand daisies—yellow, orange and

Pollie Pollard at the southern entrance to the
Valley of Death.

white. Patches of grass, fresh, green and lush, come to life, growing knee high in a fortnight or less. Weather-scarred succulents burst out in bloom, and the ashbush takes on a sheen of silvery grey.

As we continued northwards across the stony wastes, we came across scattered sand dunes, their colour changing from beige to orange. To the immediate west the Jackal hills, dishevelled and sand-bedecked, rose into view. An hour later we drew up at Dabaras, an outpost overlooking the Orange river. After a meal of rump steak roasted by Pollard over thorntree embers, we moved on into the sands.

Beyond Dabaras the desert climbs into a range of hills and then tumbles into an immense valley, one so eerie in appearance, so deathly desolate as to send shivers snaking along the spine. As far as our eyes could reach into the hazy horizon, the valley seemed to be writhing and somersaulting in an agony of craters, cliffs, chasms and peaks. There was not a hint of a breeze, not a sound except the croaking lament of a flight of crows gliding in the distance towards us. Our nostrils filled with the fetid smell of hot stagnant air. Our mouths tasted of dust.

Jackal
Canyon.

'A valley of death,' I said to Pollard.

'No, not death,' he replied, 'not if you know it as I do. On the contrary, this valley teems with life—hyena, jackal, skunk and meerkat, not to mention puff-adders, horned adders and uncountable colonies of desert rats. And what looks like a jumble of landscapes now transforms into a blaze of colour in the spring.'

Farther to the north we crept out of the valley on to a dune plateau stretched out to the western horizon. Towards evening we returned to Dabaras, and during the following two days made a study of the plants and shrubs in the immediate vicinity. Among the many shown me by Pollard was the Namib milk-bush, a sour-leafed shrub some three metres tall. Its stems compact and leathery, it serves the gemsbok as a protective screen when the sand winds rage. The gemsbok also relish its roots, scraping them out of the dunes with their hoofs.

On our fourth and final day together Pollard and I set out from Dabaras in a south-easterly direction, bound for nearby Jackal Canyon. We joined a track that accompanies a dried-up river bed, zigzagging through uprooted trees and thickets of black ebony, and reaching a chasm walled on either side by an entanglement of rock pinnacles fully a hundred metres high. Suddenly we were in the heart of Jackal Canyon, the cliffs growing gradually taller, the heat mounting rapidly and here and there the sun cutting swathes of light into the inky shadows.

A little ahead of us the pinnacles converged, and looking up we noticed their sides were splashed white with the droppings of a colony of black eagles. Nests two metres across hung over row upon row of ledges jutting out from the cliffs. Then a male eagle emerged from a nest and glared at us with menacing eyes. Its neck outstretched, beak opened wide, for a fleeting moment I believed it was poised to tear us apart. Several more came circling in to roost, filling the canyon with discordant shrieks. So we remained in the truck studying their movements through binoculars, and marvelling at the ear-rending cacophony that now pervaded the canyon. It was a relief to our ears when eventually we withdrew from the spot and retraced our tracks through the avenue of pinnacles. According to Pollard, the Nama say that no one would dare enter Jackal Canyon at night for fear of Hottentot ghosts. Fewer still would aspire to visiting it by day, were they to come upon black eagles during their mating time, as we had done.

Koebus and the Valley of Stones

Pollie Pollard's foreman at Beauvallon farm was Gideon Louw, a middle-aged, half-breed Nama with features that bore witness to far more than a trace of white ancestry. Short, thick-set and of a quiet disposition, he came from Koebus, the Nama settlement I was due to visit. So when I was told by Pollard on our return to the farm that Gideon had agreed to be my guide, I knew instinctively that my trip to Koebus would turn out well. Gideon, like Pollard and D'Arcy Henry of Palapye, was the kind of man one was glad to have at one's side in the desert.

We departed for Koebus three days later at dawn. We set off by jeep along the southern banks of the Orange river, then veering north-eastwards continued for about forty kilometres through unchanging Namaqualand scrub. There were no signs of human life along the road, except two tiny shepherds' shanties built of corrugated tin and adjoined by a wired-off sheep pen. To the south-east overshadowing the entire horizon lay the purple-black Rugterveld mountain range, and straight ahead at its feet, the Valley of Stones, domain of the Nama of Koebus.

When the American astronauts reached the moon in 1969, their first sight of its surface must have resembled the scene of abject desolation that was to meet my eyes, as we descended into the valley on that mid-morning in June. Before us lay a sea of powdery sand, strewn with stones ranging in size from marbles to cricket balls. Pallid, unliving dunes, rippled by the play of the winds; distant Nama Hottentot huts dotted like fly-specks on a kitchen ceiling. This was the Valley of Stones.

Driving over a rise into a long, shallow hollow, the nearest Nama settlement hove into view, a simple rectangular shack and three tiny dome-shaped huts beside it. Not a tree in sight. Only four little homes in the heart of nothingness.

On reaching the shack we were met by the headman or *korporaal*, as he preferred to be called, of Koebus. He was a short, spare little man with a broad, flat face, narrow jaws and a receding chin. Dressed in an open-necked shirt, brown trousers and black shoes he proffered a small limp hand, introducing himself as Gert Swartbooi. When I asked his permission to visit his people in the Valley of Stones, he chuckled: considering the Nama were backward desert folk, he could not imagine of what interest they could be to a white man from far-off Johannesburg. As this was my wish, however, he would suggest that Gideon take me first to the home of old Adam Obies, the best-known Nama this side of the Rugterveld range.

Obies's settlement consisted of two little huts, built side by side, one for cooking in and one for sleeping in. Made of woven mats in traditional style, and patched here and there with sacking and sheets of tin, each of the structures was weighted down with a single thong flung over the dome, and attached on either side to a heavy stone. Close by, in a pen not four metres wide, old Obies kept a handful of karakul sheep. There was also a platform of sticks built on supporting poles, where his fowls roosted at night out of reach of dogs, meerkats and jackals. We found

Valley of Stones.

Nama settlement.

Paul Swartbooi, an elder of Koebus.

Nama karakul sheep.

Old Obies.

Sarah, Obies's wife.

Adam Obies seated on a stool in the shade of the cooking hut, and beside him his wife Sarah. With drooping shoulders, shrivelled and sallow with age, she was dishing up porridge into enamel plates for their morning meal.

Like most Nama men Obies was small, very small. He had deep-set restless eyes, brown like hazelnuts, and his chin and cheeks were covered in stubble. He wore a blue headcloth, a slouch hat, and around his neck a multi-coloured scarf tied at the side in a crude knot. Dressed in a khaki shirt, a soiled grey jacket, baggy pants and homemade shoes, he appeared greatly over-burdened with clothes for one permanently subjected to the intense heat of the valley. At a glance he looked about seventy. He was a sickly man and, according to Gideon, his physique was a mere shadow of what it had been during the prime of his life. Rising from the stool and leaning on a stick he came slowly towards us. By the way he was forced to measure each step, I guessed he was in pain.

'It's no good,' he said on reaching us, 'I've never been the same since that leopard got me; but then neither has the leopard been the same.'

He then burst into hearty laughter, and shaking our hands said he was glad we had come.

'Leopard?' I queried.

'Yes,' cried Obies, 'on the banks of the Great river,' and he pointed with his stick to the north.

'It almost killed me,' he added, 'and for sure it would have, had I not done the killing first.'

Now he laughed again, louder and longer, and drawing a long-bladed knife from under his belt, held it point downwards, stabbing the air.

'This is what saved me,' he said.

At Obies's invitation we repaired to the shade of the cooking hut, and sitting down beside him asked him to tell us the story.

During his younger days, old Adam began, he was the most skilful hunter and trapper in the valley, having captured and killed more leopards than any other Nama of his time. Some ten years back he was visited one evening at sundown by goatherds with news that an uncommonly large leopard had been caught in his trap at the Orange river. According to them it had died of exhaustion after struggling for hours.

Hurrying northwards Obies had reached the trap in gathering dusk. He found the leopard outstretched in the reeds, its left foreleg gripped high in the jaws of the trap and much of its body covered in blood. He had not the slightest doubt it was dead, but having learned from a lifetime of trapping never to underrate the cunning of leopards, he prodded its body with a hunting stick. It showed no sign of life. There was nothing to fear.

Nama hunter.

Obies had barely knelt down beside the leopard to disengage its leg from the trap when suddenly it whiplashed to its feet with a roar, and turning on its captor sank its jaws into his left upper arm. Obies was flung on to his back; and the agonized beast, releasing its grip, pounced on top of him, attacking viciously, and clawing long gashes into his chest, stomach and thighs.

Now, as Obies struggled for his life, his thoughts moved in a flash to the knife in his belt, and at the first opportunity he drew it and plunged it into the leopard's side. Next moment he was free and sank crumpled into the reeds, his mind swimming with visions of approaching death. He could not recall how long he

From Obies's place Gideon and I headed southwards through the valley calling on settlements and entering into discussions with the Nama, some of them old and typically Hottentot in appearance, others young and conspicuously hybridized. In the shadows of the Rugterveld range, we came upon a small circle of adults weeping at the door of a hut, their heads bowed low, and faces held in their hands. One of the group coming forward to greet us explained that his grandmother, Fredrika, was gravely ill and seemed to be dying. As he and his companions had considered our sudden and unexpected arrival an important omen, he asked that we follow him into the old woman's hut and join her family in prayer.

We found old Fredrika stretched out on the floor, her wasted body wrapped in blankets, her face shrunken and deathly pallid peeping from out of a cloth that covered her head. There was not a flicker of expression in her cavernous eyes as we knelt down beside her. Fredrika, we were to learn, was both blind and deaf. In recent months her legs had become too weak to hold her and now her time to die had come. All that remained was for her dear ones to pray that she would be taken gently into the shades of departed souls where, according to Nama belief, life is eternal and the stresses of senility unknown.

Leaving old Fredrika's hut and the circle of grief-stricken friends outside, we continued through the valley over rolling dunes, through eroded hollows and across vast stretches of stone. My aim was to assess to what extent customs and beliefs had changed as a result of contact between the Nama and white men.

During the following two days we spent much of our time with Jan Josef, Obies's friend, for as one of the oldest and reputedly the wisest members of the small community, he was ideally suited to answer my questions and add to the findings I had noted. Like Obies he was a sickly old man, arthritic and dropsical, but nevertheless eager to assist. In the discussions I had with him it soon became apparent he had seen considerable changes take place in the way of life of the Nama.

'These days,' he said a little forlornly, 'many of our people lack pride in the way they live. Just look at our huts. When I was a child our parents were craftsmen, and in order to weave roof mats of the very best quality they would travel great distances along the banks of the Great river in search of the tallest and strongest reeds. They would never have used sacks, cardboard and flattened tin for roofs as some of us do. That would have meant they were backward.

'And you can go through this valley from hut to hut, and you'll find few items of furniture made these days by the people themselves. The old Nama *katel* or bedstead, for instance, carved from tree trunks and strung with skin straps, no longer

Jan Josef.

lay there waiting to die, but it must have been almost midnight when gradually he became aware first of voices beside him, then the light of a lantern and finally the face of his closest friend, a fellow trapper called Jan Josef.

'With the help of the goatherds who had led him to the trap,' continued Obies, 'Jan Josef carried me back to the Valley of Stones, and for five long months I lay in bed, my torn body burning with pain.

'Just look at this mess,' he grinned, unbuttoning his shirt and trousers and exposing a scar-twisted torso and disfigured left hip. 'This is what happens when you're caught unawares by the spotted devil.'

Nama settlement near the Rugterveld range.

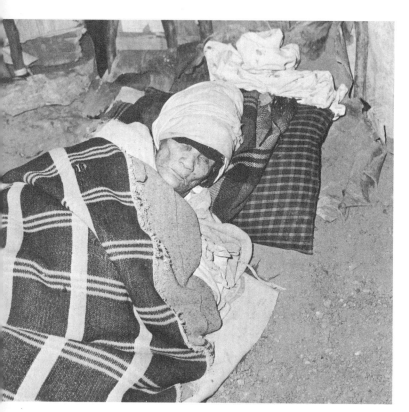

Fredrika's passing.

exists, for today our people want only the white man's kind of bed, and if they're too poor they sleep on the ground.

'It's too much trouble for the young ones to make those wooden stools we used to make; too much trouble to fetch clay from the river for making pots, when there are enamel utensils and metal buckets to be bought at our trading store. Too much trouble to carve spoons from wood, as the old people did, or to weave baskets or even to flay skins for karosses. Everything today is too much trouble.'

'Does that mean you would prefer to keep your water in ostrich egg-shells as you used to do,' I asked teasingly, 'and to smoke your tobacco in sawn-off antelope femur bones, instead of the modern pipe I notice you have? And what about bows and arrows; would you prefer to use them for hunting instead of a rifle or shotgun?'

'No, that's different,' Jan Josef replied, 'because guns are very much better than Nama weapons. But just think of the food we eat these days. Can you tell me that the bread we buy at the trading store, and eat every day until our stomachs swell, compares with the many kinds of wild berries, fruits, roots and bulbs we once collected right here in the desert, on the slopes of the Rugterveld mountains?

Jan Josef's huts.

Above left Middle-aged Nama woman near Koebus.

Above right Little Boelie.

'I can remember the beer we brewed from honey and the feeling of happiness it gave us inside. Now the Nama drink European liquors that turn their heads, and make them fight each other and even kill. No, many of these new things may be good for white men, but they haven't always been good for the Nama.'

Asking Jan Josef if he thought all aspects of European culture had had an adverse effect on his people, he replied with an emphatic 'No!'

'No,' he repeated, 'there is much we Nama are thankful for, and the greatest of all is education. For a long time now our young people have been attending school, and by learning to read and write they have made their parents proud of them. The schools and the teachings of the white man's church have up-lifted us and helped to rid our minds of superstitions. Much of the fears caused by our belief in harmful ghosts, or in the powers of witches and the evil doings of sorcerers, no longer burden our minds. Not that magic and witchcraft are no longer practised in the valley. They are in parts. It is just that we also have the white man's Christ to turn to in times of trouble.'

After two days in Koebus and its Valley of Stones Gideon and I bade Jan Josef, old Obies and Gert Swartbooi, the *korporaal*, farewell and withdrew westwards bound for Oranjemund. We drove past flocks of goats and karakul sheep, a party of Nama youths and maidens dancing on a dune to the strains of a concertina, and a convoy of donkey carts stacked high with firewood fetched from the banks of the Orange river.

Reflecting on the turbulent history of the Hottentot peoples, the Khoi-Khoin or Men of Men the Dutch had met at the Cape, my thoughts returned again to the Nama of Koebus, and I wondered what the Fates had in store for them. Although their roots reach deeper into the soil than any of the major Southern African peoples, I had a feeling they might shrivel in the course of time in that lonely Valley of Stones.

North of the Namib Desert

The OvaHimba

On the morning after my visit to Koebus I flew by Dakota from Kortdoring airport to the northern reaches of South-West Africa. There were forty-two Ovambo mine-workers aboard, all returning home after working under contract for several months on the diamond fields. For the first few hundred kilometres we followed the Skeleton Coast. We then turned north-eastwards over Walvis Bay, across the Namib Desert and Etosha pan, landing in Ondongwa in the late afternoon. The flight had lasted almost five hours.

I was met at the Ondongwa airstrip by Herman Grobler, a local resident with whom arrangements had been made to take me by truck to the tribes of Ovamboland. There was also a giant of a man called Blackie Swart, a friend of Grobler's, who I learned would be accompanying us.

From Ondongwa we drove to Oshakati, where we spent the night. Next morning we set out westwards for the Kunene river which defines the border between South-West Africa and Angola. We made our first stop on the left bank of the river, overlooking the Ruacana falls. Having travelled for some fifty kilometres across flat and bleak countryside studded with towering anthills and *omulungu*, or ivory palms, we covered the remaining twenty-three kilometres through valleys and hills that were layered with a dense growth of *mopani*, *marulla* and *baobab* tree. Although in the throes of winter, this part of the territory was still hot and sultry and infested with tantalizing swarms of gnats and *mopani* flies.

In a valley not a stone's throw from the falls we came upon the OvaHimba, a nomadic Negro people said to number no more than twelve thousand in all South-West Africa. Virtually untouched by Western culture—for over a century they have stubbornly turned their backs on missionaries seeking to work among them—the OvaHimbas' way of life has undergone few changes since ancient times. They are by tradition goat- and cattle-breeders but, like other nomadic peoples of our western regions, derive much of their diet from veldfoods and insects collected by the womenfolk, and game and birds snared or trapped by the men.

The OvaHimba are a handsome people, the males generally tall and athletically built and the women petite. Facial features are typical Negroid. There is evidence, however, of an Hamitic, Arab or Semitic strain, as revealed by the high-bridged noses some of them have. The OvaHimba smile is interesting, for in accordance with age-old custom the lower incisors are removed at the time of puberty, and the upper ones notched in the shape of moth wings.

The OvaHimba notch the upper incisors in the shape of moth wings.

The womenfolk style their hair into dozens of plaited strings. The frill of goat skin on top of the head is worn by married women.

Opposite page OvaHimba hunting and fighting spears are short and light, the shafts fitted with the tail of the wildebeest.

OvaHimba warriors wear necklaces made of lead and whelk shell beads. The white, circular amulet is also made of whelk shell. Note the cylindrical snuff box, amulet and knife attached to the belt, and the sandals strapped to the ankles.

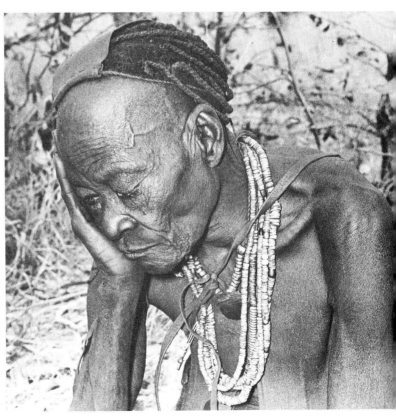

Some of the hair plaits are threaded with lead beads.

OvaHimba mother breastfeeding her child.

OvaHimba great-grandmother, blind with age.

OvaHimba warrior, Ruacana falls. Beneath his oily turban are two huge plaits of hair fixed with a mixture of butter and red ochre. The spoon-like implement over his left temple is a scalp scratcher.

adorned with beads carved from whelk shell and lead, and in the case of married women are topped with a frill of goat skin.

Unyieldingly conservative, the OvaHimba have clung assiduously to age-old modes of dress. They have shunned, for example, the multi-coloured beads and trinkets brought by pioneer European traders into South-West Africa, continuing to fashion their belts, necklaces, wrist and ankle bands out of leather studded with homemade beads. The most popular ornament worn both by men and women is a large whelk shell amulet, which hangs like a pendant from around the neck.

The use of animal fat as a skin lubricant is widely practised in tribal Southern Africa. The OvaHimba, however, have an obsession for butter and ochre, smearing the mixture not only into their hair and on their ornaments, but also over face, torso and limbs. This, they say, serves as protection against the vicious South-West African sun, but more important, as one young woman put it, it is as essential to their appearance as are feathers to a bird. Even their clothes are daubed with butter and ochre— the goatskin kilts worn by the men and the heavy calfskin aprons worn fore and aft by the women. Even sandals and snuff-boxes. Everything.

Huts and Kraals

The OvaHimba live in tiny kraals comprising no more than three or four huts facing inwards on to a cattlefold. Conical-shaped, these huts are built of staves packed side by side and supported by a central vertical pole. They are plastered on the outside with a mixture of cowdung and clay, which forms a solid, waterproof crust when dry. There are no windows, and the narrow, solitary entrance is shut at nights with oxhide, goatskin or woven reed mats. Like most nomadic peoples the OvaHimba have few possessions—earthen cooking utensils, oxhide milk and butter bags, wooden pails, hunting sticks, spears and, of course, their clothing and ornaments.

Cattle play an important role in OvaHimba culture, not only as a source of food supply and raw materials for clothes and utensils, but also as a determining factor in the status enjoyed by the owners. A man's wealth, for example, is determined by the size of his herd, no matter how inferior the quality. This means

Dress and Ornaments

Like most other tribes the OvaHimba have distinctive hairstyles. The men wear single or double plaits, long and thick, and fixed with a mixture of butter and brick-coloured ochre. The women on the other hand do their hair in dozens of plaited strings which hang loosely over the shoulders and back, and are just as generously daubed with butter and ochre. These are sometimes that beasts are seldom if ever slaughtered specifically for meat. Oxen are, however, slaughtered from time to time for sacrifice to the spirit world, as a token either of thanksgiving or of repentance, depending on a number of circumstances. The wider the span of a beast's horns the greater its value, so only short-horned oxen are slaughtered for sacrificial purposes.

Death and Burial

Because of the simple and secluded life they lead, the Ova-Himba are steeped in superstition. They seem far more apprehensive of death than most other Southern African tribes, despite their strict adherence to the spirit cult. This stems to a certain degree from their somewhat confused concept of the soul. Some see it vaguely as a mysterious force that inhabits the spine, keeping the body erect in life and leaving it immobile and subject to decay in death. Others claim it is housed in the blood, which accounts for its clogging when death occurs, or a wound is made. Indeed, blood severed from the bodily stream, as in the case of menstruation, is considered defiled, and therefore fraught with evil influences, which must be removed by way of purificatory ritual.

When death follows on illness, it is not always accepted by the OvaHimba as a natural consequence. Invariably a child's dying is attributed either to sorcery or to the workings of an angry ancestor, especially if the parents are known as transgressors. Sinful or even irresponsible youths are the ones most prone to be robbed of their earthly lives. This serves as a stabilizing factor in the way they behave, for in the realm of ancestors a youthful spirit has little claim to status. Greyheads alone can look forward to a position of importance in the life that comes after death.

Burial follows soon after death. The corpse is bound in a crouching position with strips of *mopani* bark, and then lowered together with personal belongings into the grave. The funeral of an important man is usually accompanied by the killing of an ox. Its nostrils are stuffed with chunks of clay and its snout held closed by dozens of powerful hands. When eventually it falls senseless to the ground, it is pounced upon by handpicked mourners who break its neck. It is then skinned and dismembered, and an offering of the flesh is made to the ancestral spirits. The mourners pray long and fervently, and when the service ends and the grave has been filled with soil, the ox's horns are placed beside it. This spot now becomes hallowed ground for use in the years ahead as a shrine or place of worship. Usually it is marked with a stout pole at the head of the grave, or with stones packed close together over the heap.

Kukuri's Kraal

OvaHimba families are grouped into bands, and like the Bushmen they delight in congregating among the thorntrees, the men and women sitting apart, and the children romping close by in the veld. In contrast to the Bushmen, who are by nature shy and reserved in the presence of strangers, the OvaHimba tend to be rowdy. In fact, whilst working among them I found it difficult to question people in the hubbub of chatter and laughter.

Among the kraals we visited near the Ruacana falls was one that appealed to me far more than the others. Perhaps it was because of its picturesque setting between two *baobab* trees, or perhaps it was the special liking I had for its owner, a tall young man named Kukuri who stood out among the rest as intelligent and willing to answer any questions. Kukuri had only two huts, but unlike most of his neighbours he had erected a circular enclosure where the cooking was done by his wife, Harero.

It was there that we met Harero. She was a short, small-boned woman who had had twins six months before, bringing joy to herself and her husband and, indeed, to the rest of their band. Seeing the babies on the ground beside her, I recalled that in generations past the birth of twins in some parts of tribal Southern Africa had been considered an unfavourable omen. In order to avoid impending misfortune, or even disaster, it had been the custom for the younger of the two to be put to death and then to be buried in a broken earthen pot. Until such time as the mother had been ritually cleansed, she would have been shunned by her friends, and particularly by expectant mothers lest they too should become defiled. She would have been kept in strict isolation until declared purged of contamination by a medicine man.

According to some elderly people I questioned at Ruacana with Kukuri's assistance, infanticide had never been practised by the OvaHimba. The birth of a child, I was told, is made possible by the Great One who governs all forms of life. Therefore killing a twin would mean arousing the Great One's wrath and, indeed, coming into conflict with the whole spirit world.

My presence at Kukuri's kraal attracted about fifteen inquisitive members of his band to the huts. Some of them, so Kukuri informed me, had become suspicious because of the questions I had asked about OvaHimba customs and beliefs. The older people were baffled at the inspection I made and the photographs I took of foodstuffs, grinding stones, utensils, weapons, amulets and, in fact, every aspect of their material culture. However when the time arrived to leave and I gave them tobacco, sweets and money, they insisted that henceforth we should visit them regularly. In order to delay our departure, they further insisted that we witness a mock battle between

Kukuri, renowned as a stick fighter. Note the carved headrest or OvaHimba 'pillow' attached to his belt.

two rival groups of braves, in a clearing among the trees.

So for twenty minutes we were entertained to a display of stick fighting. Although it had begun in a spirit of fun, it was not long before tempers flared and the braves were involved in a brawl. And all the while the clatter of their sticks was accompanied by the shrilling of the women, the caterwauling and the ear-piercing shrills that came from flat, oval-shaped, metal whistles wedged between the notched incisors of a party of herdsmen and blown with force. When the fighting came to an end, and the excitement was over, we loaded my cameras into Herman Grobler's truck. As slowly we drew away, Kukuri and his companions crowded around us, singing and kicking up dust in a lively dance.

Ovamboland

In contrast to the hilly and wooded Ruacana area, central Ovamboland, in the region of Oshakati, is flat and sandy and seemingly barren during the dry month of June. Dotted with trees, palms, lofty anthills and an occasional muddy pool, it has a special charm of its own.

The Ovambo nation is divided into eight kindred tribes (the Ombalantu, Ondonga, Ongandjera, Oukwanyama, Uukolonkadhi, Eunda, Uukwalundhi and Uukwambi) each ruled by a chieftain, each speaking the same language (with minor differences in dialect) and each pursuing an almost identical way of life. At the same time as my visit to South-West Africa, the nation's political head was Ushona Shimi, senior councillor of the Ovamboland executive council, and chief of the Ongandjera tribe. It was with his blessing that I researched in kraals north, south and east of Oshakati, accompanied again by Grobler and Swart. Towards the end of June we arrived by truck at Ombala, royal kraal of an Uukwambi chieftain named Ashipala Ipinge. We were met at the main gates by the chief himself, a lean middle-aged man, suave and smiling, and simply dressed in khaki shorts and shirt.

Uukwambi Royal Kraal

Whereas in other parts of Ovambo territory I had directed my researches mainly to aspects of ritual, now in Chief Ipinge's district I decided to study the local ecology, the crops cultivated, and, in fact, every aspect of the Uukwambi diet. My choice of locality could not have been better.

Ipinge's kraal followed roughly the pattern to be found throughout Ovamboland. There were eighteen huts, eleven circular and the remainder rectangular or square. They were built of *mopani* stems packed firmly together and plastered on the inner side with anthill clay. Roofs were conical-shaped and thickly thatched with sorghum stems from the harvested fields. The huts were grouped into seven sections, each isolated from the rest by hedges made from sticks or poles, and bound together with *mopani* bark. Winding in and out of the kraal was a labyrinth of connecting passages, built of the same materials. Some, I noticed, were in need of repair, as a result of the constant flow of human traffic. The most elaborate section of an Uukwambi kraal, as I was to discover at Ombala, is the patriarch's quarters, for it is here that he sleeps, entertains his more intimate friends, and is able to enjoy a leisurely hour or two on his own without disturbance. In addition to his sleeping hut he has a similar structure for storing clothes, weapons and smaller

Entrance to Chief Ipinge's kraal.

Sleeping quarters of Chief Ipinge's male children.

personal effects, another for pots, ladles, strainers and other essentials for brewing beer, and finally a creamery and pantry and a special dwelling for guests.

Adjoining Chief Ipinge's quarters and immediately within the main entrance of the kraal was the *olupale* or gathering place. It consisted of an open-sided structure supported on poles and with a thatched roof. This was furnished with crude tree-trunk benches and was used exclusively by men. Close by was a tall circular palisade where the sacred fire, believed to be symbolic of man's spiritual perpetuity, was kept permanently alight by attendants working in shifts.

Other important features of the Ombala kraal were separate quarters for each of the chief's wives, and communal huts to house, respectively, his adolescent children and retainers. There was also a special enclosure where harvested sorghum was stored in granaries for day-to-day use and another for cooking, and adjacent to these an additional two, one for women and the other for men, where meals were served.

Chief Ipinge's senior wife.

Durra or sorghum millet,
the most important crop
in Ovamboland.

Uukwambi Crops

The Ovambo are predominantly agriculturalists, cultivating mainly a species of coarse sorghum millet called *durra*. Most patriarchs have large threshing floors made of anthill clay—at Ombala there was one inside the kraal itself, and another centrally situated among the lands—and the harvests are stored in huge, spherical granaries. These were made of pliable *mopani* sticks bound with *mopani* bark, and supported on four-legged wooden frames. Each granary was sheltered from the rains by a pointed, movable roof fixed to a circle of upright poles. Not far from the main kraal gates was the palisade cattlefold, and beside it two or three drinking troughs carved from the trunks of the ivory palm.

Of all the tribes of Southern Africa, few are as abundantly endowed with both indigenous and cultivated foods as the peoples of Ovamboland. The most popular crops, apart from sorghum, are beans, groundnuts, pumpkins, melons and an edible calabash, and within the kraals, growing over the hedges, climber gourds.

The planting season begins with the coming of the first soaking rains in October. On an appointed day the kraal patriarch presents his wives with sorghum seed for sowing. He then accompanies them to the *olupale* or gathering place, or sometimes to the sacred fire, where together they make offerings to the ancestral spirits, beseeching them to keep watch over the crops from the time of planting until the harvests are stored.

At Ombala, according to Chief Ipinge, his wives, like other Uukwambi women in the district, do the sowing by hand, scattering the sorghum seed widely, then digging it into the soil with hoes. The sowers work in groups, now chanting or humming a tribal ditty, now chattering or laughing together, and always keeping a look out for fowls, doves, finches and starlings that sneak continually into the fields.

Planting continues throughout November and into December, for after the sorghum come the beans, groundnuts, pumpkins, melons and gourds. Meanwhile thick carpets of weeds spring up everywhere threatening to throttle the sprouting crops. So at the first opportunity the women, assisted by their teenage daughters, move in with hoes. Among the many tasks they have to perform, weeding is the one that accounts for most of their time in the months ahead.

When the sorghum is ready for reaping in June members of kraals, mindful of the damage that can be done to the crops by swarms of ravenous *quelea* finches, start gathering the harvest without delay. On arrival at Ombala we watched Chief Ipinge's reapers at work. Ripened ears of sorghum, stripped by the men from the shrivelled plants, were being packed into baskets.

Granaries are made of *mopani* staves bound with *mopani* bark. They are plastered inside with a mixture of cowdung and anthill clay.

Uukwambi hoes and storage basket.

When granaries have been filled with sorghum
millet, they are covered with conical roofs
supported on a circule of poles.

These were then lifted on to the heads of the women and taken
to the threshing floors. Back and forth the women strode in file,
pausing now and then to enjoy a draught of sorghum beer, or to
breastfeed a baby in the shade of the thorntrees.

The threshing had been started some days before by a party
of women. They worked gaily together in the mellow warmth
of the sun, singing in harmony, as with long, heavy-headed
pestles they rhythmically pounded the sorghum packed in heaps
on the threshing floors. Most of the time their feet were enveloped in puffs of chaff, and when periodically they paused to
rest, covered from head to foot in sorghum dust, they would
emerge powdery-white, looking a little like ghosts.

Uukwambi maiden threshing
sorghum millet.

Fishing and Trapping

In the Uukwambi district, when the threshing has been done the winnowing starts. The grain is then taken in baskets to the granaries, both inside and outside the kraals. This marks the time not only for rejoicing and thanksgiving but also for harvesting the beans, groundnuts, melons and other crops. Thereafter, until the spring rains come, there is much to be done in and around the kraals. There are hut floors and hedges that need repairing, new baskets, platters and fish traps to be woven and new wooden utensils to be carved.

During the summer months an extraordinary phenomenon occurs in Ovamboland. A thin sheet of floodwater moves tardily over the countryside from rain-swollen water courses in the north, filling dams, pools and pans and bringing in its flow great quantities of fish, frogs and crabs. So while the women take care of the lands, tilling, planting and weeding, men, youths, boys and maidens busy themselves with fishing and trapping. This is a popular pastime which continues through the rainy season, day in and day out, from sunrise to sunset and often until well after dark.

The men are particularly skilled with hook and line, even though much of their tackle is homemade and by conventional standards inadequate. And they are expert at spearing, especially in areas where pools are plentiful and where sheatfish and mud-wallowing barbel abound. By far the majority of Uukwambi, however, take part in trapping not only because it is easy to do but also because it allows for group participation, which in turn is conducive to conviviality.

The height of the trapping season is reached when the flood-waters arrive, and again when they start to recede in autumn. In Uukwambi territory I saw mud walls built knee high across selected pools and channels, each with interspersing gaps through which the waters were made to flow. Covering these gaps were rows of sticks dug firmly into the mud and interwoven with a network of twigs and reeds. By this simple device the fish were trapped inside or outside the pools, and were therefore easy to catch either by hand or in baskets, depending on the depth of the water.

Much of the catching at Chief Ipinge's kraal and, indeed, in most parts of Ovamboland was done with a funnel-shaped plunging-basket woven from pliable twigs. Open at the base it

Chief Ipinge's senior wife winnowing sorghum millet.

After the winnowing the sorghum chaff is brushed together, and then used as a cattle feed.

The carcasses of birds, and the flesh of game are salted and dried for consumption during the austere winter months.

Below In the shallow pools around Ovambo kraals, the women catch fish with plunging baskets, and the men and boys with homemade rods.

has a lateral hole near the top, just large enough for a fair-sized hand and arm to enter with ease. Used almost exclusively by women, the plunging-basket, held at the apex, was dipped at random into the muddy bottom of shallow pools. At the slightest splutter within the funnel the women knew a fish had been trapped, so they would pause, reach down through the hole and remove the catch. This they would fling to a companion on the banks near by, where it was clubbed to death and disembowelled. The plunging method, although popular, has one unpleasant feature: often within minutes of entering a pool the women would find their legs and arms so infested with leeches, that they were compelled to withdraw from the water and scrape them off. It was a source of amazement to me that in spite of this they kept on returning to the water, seemingly undeterred by the constant onslaught of these objectionable creatures.

Apart from their daily consumption of freshly caught fish in the rainy season, I noticed that the Uukwambi had also been stocking up supplies for the winter. Between April and June much of the catch had been cleaned, generously sprinkled with coarse salt dug from salt pans in the south and packed on hut roofs to dry. Other flesh foods had been dehydrated in similar fashion—frogs collected in great quantities by herdboys, and a variety of waterfowl, including teal, wild goose, heron and red-knobbed coot, clubbed to death on the banks of pools, or in the sedges under cover of darkness.

Hunting

A food that has virtually disappeared from the Uukwambi diet is venison. There was a time when game abounded in all Ovambo territories—giraffe, kudu, eland, springbok and numerous smaller species of antelope. Hunting, snaring and trapping had been as much a part of Ovambo custom as the planting of crops and the brewing of beer. Today most of the game has been wiped out, and from what I saw in Uukwambi territory much of the hunting, snaring and trapping is confined to the lesser mammals such as hares, spring hares, field mice, rats and moles. Veld birds were hunted by teenage boys using wooden arrows fired from bows made of palm-leaf stalk. The little

Arrows for bird hunting, carved from wood.

Self-sown indigenous watermelons play an
important part in the Ovambo diet.

Ovamboland has a large variety of indigenous wild fruits.

Ovambo girls spend much of their time collecting edible fruits and berries in the surroundings.

hunting the adults still did was with iron-tipped arrows smeared with poison, and fired with a heavy bow fashioned from thorn-tree staves.

It was interesting to note that apart from the fish and frogs they caught and the birds and animals they hunted the Uuk-wambi had access to other protein foods in the surrounding velds. For example, they considered white ants and termites a delicacy, especially when roasted and mixed with butter, ground-nuts and sprinklings of salt. Equally popular were the rissoles they made from dried locusts or grasshoppers, and the stews they prepared from *mopani* caterpillars, mixed with beans and wild spinach.

Marulla Wine

Nature is particularly kind to the Uukwambi in late summer when the fruits of the *marulla*, wild fig and other indigenous trees mature. There were trees on the outskirts of Chief Ipinge's kraal called *eenyandi* which bore fruit just as abundantly as the *marulla*. The fruit of *eenyandi* looked not unlike miniature tomatoes, except that they were yellow and hard, and sweeter and more pleasant to the palate. Collected in baskets and stored in the huts, they were relished from morning till night by the women and children.

During the *marulla* season, which falls roughly between the beginning of February and the end of March, work in Ovambo-land tends to be regarded as out of fashion. Not so much because the people are waiting for the sorghum to mature, or that there is nothing else for them to do. It is just that when the *marulla* ripen the fruit falls to the ground, and this means it has to be collected and taken in baskets to the kraals. For the fruit of the *marulla* can be turned into wine as delicious as the very best made from grapes, but far more potent and thirst-evoking. During *marulla* time, *marulla* wine flows continually into bottles, pots and gourds, and thence into a multitude of craving mouths, from the Okavango river to the Ruacana falls. Everyone drinks homemade wine at *marulla* time except, of course, infants and children. But even they join in the fun of *marulla* time, cautiously keeping beyond arm's length of their tipsy elders, whose tempers, they have learnt, become progressively shorter as the fruit keeps falling from the trees.

Whereas *marulla* wine is a seasonal drink, and sorghum beer a permanent feature of the Ovambo diet, I was to learn that in Uukwambi territory mead is a delicacy served only on special occasions to special guests. This seemed strange considering that honey was so plentiful throughout the district, and the brew so avidly relished. The reason, I discovered, was that in South-

The Uukwambi have
tiny cattle that
yield only small
quantities of milk.

West Africa bees become abnormally vicious at the height of the honey season, and that no more than a handful of kraal owners would dare to tamper with swarms hived in the hollows of tree trunks, abandoned antbear (ant-eater) holes and similar inaccessible places. Like *marulla* wine, Uukwambi mead is stored in earthen vessels, corked with stoppers carved from wood, and sealed with anthill clay.

Dwarf-like Cattle

Although primarily tillers and planters, the Ovambo tribes are also cattle-breeders and, like the Tswana in the east, have cattle-posts throughout the more wooded regions where grazing is plentiful during winter months. The Uukwambi cattle were the quaintest I had seen in Southern Africa, a dwarf-like species that reached no higher than a herdsman's waist. Tiny horns, tiny hooves and udders about the size of an ostrich egg. In fact, everything was small about Uukwambi cattle, including the sound of their lowing in the cattlefolds. The milking was done

Bark is stripped from *mopani* saplings and wound into balls to be used as ropes.

Boys entering adolescence are responsible for the milking. Pails are made of palm tree stems, funnels from gourds and the milk containers from calabashes bound with *mopani* bark and palm leaves.

An Uukwambi herdboy tending his charges in
the shade of a baobab tree.

Butter is made by jerking a calabash of cream
back and forth.

twice daily, at sunrise and sunset, by the younger herdboys using pails carved from the trunks of ivory palms. Poured into calabashes the milk was then taken to the kraal patriarch's enclosure, and stored in the creamery hut.

At Ombala, butter was churned in an unusual way. First, cream skimmed from standing milk was poured into a huge, spherical calabash strapped with strips of palm leaf and tied together with *mopani* bark. When about three quarters full, the calabash was hung from a crossbeam of wood fitted at either end in the fork of two tree stumps planted in the ground. Two herdboys, taking up positions on opposite sides and gripping the calabash firmly by a *mopani* bark collar that embraced its neck, began jerking it back and forth. This continued for at least two hours until it could be felt the butter had set. White and unusually soft, Uukwambi butter is tasteless and considered unfit for eating. It is used by the women as a cooking fat, and as a cosmetic and skin lubricant, and in the winter months as a salve for chapped knees, ankles, heels, elbows and knuckles.

Ritual

Considering that the Uukwambi and, indeed, the Ovambo as a whole, depend so much on nature for the success of their crops, for their grazing and fishing, and for the yield of indigenous fruit-bearing trees and shrubs, it is not surprising that foods on the one hand and the seasons on the other should play a prominent role in ritual. In December, for example, when sorghum, millet and cultivated vegetables ripen in the lands, offerings of each are made to the spirit world, accompanied by incantations and prayers of thanksgiving. A similar ceremony follows the close of the reaping season. This is not only to celebrate the end of seven months' work in the fields, but also to pay homage to Kalunga, the supreme being behind the scheme of nature, without whose blessing there could have been no harvest.

Towards the end of summer even the herds are brought into Ovambo ritual. In preparation for the dry winter months ahead they are driven into the cattlefold, prayed for and sprinkled with hallowed ash, sorghum beer and a purificatory decoction made of selected herbs. In Uukwambi country this ceremony is no longer as spectacular as it was in years gone by. Once it lasted for almost a week, but now it is over within a day. It is nonetheless still considered an important occasion, opening with prayer and offerings of milk and butter to the shades of the dead. Brought to a close with singing and dancing, it is followed by a feast provided by the owners of the herds.

Craftsmanship

It would be impossible to research among the Ovambo tribes without marvelling, sooner or later, at their exceptional gift for carving, pottery and weaving. At Ombala, Chief Ipinge's kraal, I had spent most of my time studying Uukwambi foods, but what captured my interest just as much was the great variety of wooden, clay and reed utensils in which these foods were served or stored. There were separate earthen pots for grain and beans, and others for water, milk and beer. There were the woven platters already mentioned, some for sorghum porridge, some for meat and others for vegetables. No knives and forks for, to quote Chief Ipinge, not only does food taste better when eaten with the fingers, but it reaches the hungering stomach more quickly and without fuss and bother.

At Ombala, fish, wild fowl and chicken were served in wooden bowls, and the beer and wine in goblets carved from blocks of *mopani* wood. On the three occasions we were invited to share a meal with the chief, our food was dished up in clay plates reserved for guests.

The Cooking Enclosure

All cooking at Ombala was done over an open hearth bordered by a circle of heavy, homemade bricks. These served both for keeping burning wood and embers close together, and for placing the earthen pots in positions nearest the flames. All around the hearth, as the women worked with the food, there was an assortment of large wooden stirring spoons, calabash scoops, baskets, pots and ladles made of long-necked gourds. There were always scores of fowls, dogs and cats in attendance during cooking time, all vying with each other for vantage points, and always waiting for tit-bits of food that seldom if ever came their way.

The Sacred Fire

After completing my work at Ombala, I spent some time with Chief Ipinge beside the sacred fire, screened from the rest of the kraal by a palisade of *mopani* poles. As is the custom among African peoples when a parting is at hand, the chief presented me with several gifts—three woven platters, a clay dish for eggs, a wooden fish bowl, two wooden goblets, a small calabash container for *marulla* pip oil and no less than fourteen arrows

Uukwambi clay pots, grass platters and scoops made from gourds.

Ovambo men take their meals in special enclosures, apart from the womenfolk.

Uukwambi women around a communal food
pot, enjoying a midday meal.

Chief Ipinge and members of his royal village share the spiritual warmth of the sacred fire.

complete with bow and quiver. Having placed the gifts at my feet he extended his hands over the sacred fire, inviting me to do the same. Then he beckoned a small party of men to join us, and we all sat together in silence, watching the puffs of smoke that enveloped our outstretched hands. Fully three minutes passed before Ipinge spoke. Long minutes interspersed with an occasional sneeze, heavy sighs and frequent belching as a prelude to the arrival of the spirits. Then suddenly the chief began to pray.

It was a lengthy prayer reaching from the depths of his soul, the kind usually delivered to the shades when the Uukwambi sit together, united in thought and sharing the spiritual warmth of the sacred fire; the kind said by a chief on behalf of a comrade about to embark on a journey, or a visitor due to return to a far-off home. It was a prayer calling on the spirit world to keep danger away from the traveller's road, to watch over his dear ones at home and to bring them all happily together. Indeed, it was more than all these things. It was an entreaty that the one now departing should remain at Ombala at least in thought, and that he should want to return again one day.

This was Chief Ipinge's way of saying 'goodbye'.

Mozambique

Having glimpsed at some of the peoples who inhabit the western regions of Southern Africa, we move now to the east coast territories, first joining trails in Mozambique, and later others farther to the south.

The African inhabitants of Mozambique are made up of six ethnic groups—the Ronga, Djonga, Hlanganu, Bila, Nwalungu and Hlengwe—jointly known as the Tsonga. South of Mozambique are the territories of the Swazi, Zulu and Xhosa who, like their Tsonga brethren, have long been grouped in a mosaic of tribes and clans, each speaking a similar language and following an almost identical way of life.

Mozambique has been the home of the Tsonga for several centuries. In 1818 it also gave sanctuary to a horde of Zulu-speaking refugees under a chief named Soshangane, who had been put to flight by the conqueror, Shaka, king of the Zulu. Arriving in the vicinity of what is today Lourenço Marques, Soshangane fell upon the Ronga clans living there, sacking their kraals and seizing their lands. Little did he know that he was destined to play a dramatic role in altering the course of Zulu history. Indeed, in 1828, to his great surprise, Soshangane was to humble a formidable Zulu army sent by King Shaka to capture him. A remarkable feat, considering he had never been known as a military strategist, and was backed largely by untrained fighting men. His successes were triggered by the hand of fate, for Shaka's expeditionary force, the biggest ever to go north of the Pongolo river, was stricken with dysentery and the men were barely able to keep on their feet, let alone crush Soshangane's hordes. After a series of skirmishes the Zulu withdrew and went limping homewards, harried, decoyed, ambushed and relentlessly assailed along the route by the foe. Eventually they scrambled back over the Pongolo river into Zulu territory, their ranks depleted, their spirit shattered.

As a result of this disastrous expedition into Mozambique, King Shaka himself was doomed to destruction. For hardly had the news of the fiasco reached him from the north when he was murdered by his half-brother, Dingane, who then also usurped the Zulu throne.

Amigo, the Diviner, Herbalist and Exorcizer

In 1962 I set out for Mozambique to locate the sites where Soshangane's people had come to grips with the invading Zulu. West of Goba near the Swaziland border, in a valley festooned with tall, jaundice-yellow fever trees, I came upon the kraal of an elderly Tsonga named Silo Ndwandwe. His body crumpled as the result of recurring bouts of malaria, he was said to be the grandson of Ingwe, the Leopard, a warrior who had won

Amigo, diviner,
herbalist and exorcizer.

distinction fighting at Soshangane's side against King Shaka's ill-fated army. With Silo's help I was able to trace the greater part of the route taken by the Zulu in retreat from Mozambique. It was an exciting experience, much of which I was later to record in my biography of King Dingane, *Rule of Fear*.

Whilst in the Goba district I visited several kraals with Silo, most of them small but beautifully kept. However, the one I remember best was both very small and very dilapidated, not unlike its owner, a greybeard called Maziku. It was there that I learned for the first time of Victor Hugo Makumbuyo who, according to Maziku and Silo, was the best-known diviner, herbalist and exorcizer in the more southerly parts of Mozambique. Everyone called him Amigo.

In that tiny kraal I listened with relish as the two old men happily discussed, among other things, Amigo's psychic powers, his extraordinary wisdom, and above all his eccentricities. A resi-

dent of Xipamanine, an African settlement on the outskirts of Lourenço Marques, he was apparently known from Goba to the coast as 'the one who does things back to front'.

'It's strange,' Maziku explained, 'that this man should do everything the other way round. He eats with his left hand, mounts a donkey on the wrong side, milks a cow from behind, and sometimes wears trousers back to front.'

'That's right,' added Silo, 'he's a very strange man. Some people even claim he has extra eyes, an extra nose and an extra mouth at the back of his head. This, of course, is nonsense. I'm sure what they mean is that Amigo knows everything that's going on, and when he goes into trance and speaks with the tongues of spirits, it seems to them that the voice is coming from somewhere behind him.'

Although I had met and befriended numerous African psychics in all parts of Southern Africa, and had had tuition

A Tsonga kraal in the Goba district of Mozambique.

from three of the better-known practitioners of the interior—
Khotso the millionaire diviner of Lusikisiki, Makhetha of
Griqualand East and Kekana of Skilpadfontein north of
Pretoria— I decided I must meet Amigo and compare his tech-
niques with others of his trade.

So when I had completed my work in the Goba district, I
headed for Lourenço Marques, and thence to Xipamanine where
I began looking for Amigo. Everyone I spoke to claimed to
have met him, and at least half a dozen suggested I should keep
out of his way. On enquiry I learned that Amigo was so un-
predictable, and so given to fits of ill-temper, that he was likely
to cause me embarrassment.

I eventually found him in his herbalist shop, a sooty shack
built of planking and corrugated iron. It was dark and eerie
inside, as so many of these places are, but quite the strangest-
smelling I had ever come upon. Nailed to the walls, hanging from
the ceiling, littered about the floor and stacked on makeshift
counters and shelves was a multifarious agglomeration of herbs,
roots, barks, animal skulls, skins, fats, claws, feathers, jawbones,
horns, bird wings and legs, seeds, leaves and tortoise- and sea-
shells. Draped over boxes, benches and even his bicycle was an
entanglement of dried-out intestines and bladders, strung-up
snakes, fish and owl heads, strings of beetles, strings of hornet
nests, strings of salted crocodile livers, carcasses of mongoose,
lizard and iguana and, indeed, a hundred and one other bits and
pieces unfamiliar to my eyes.

Amidst the chaos was a grimy paraffin lamp, its modest flame
teasing the murky surroundings and faintly revealing the form of
an elderly African man who stood watching, rather suspiciously
I thought, wide-eyed like a startled owl.

'My father,' I said, as is the custom when a younger man greets
a greyhead, 'I have come from afar to meet Amigo.'

To which he replied, coming forward: 'Then you have found
the one you seek, but whether or not you will have the right to
stay depends on what you want of him.'

I told him I had been sent by Silo, told him about my years
of travelling to tribal peoples and told him of Khotso, Makhetha,
Kekana and other psychics by whose tutelage I had been able
to delve the depths of occultism. Amigo ventured a little smile.
He had heard of Khotso, he nodded, but not of the other two
men. Now stepping into the light, he showered me with questions
about Khotso's magical powers, claiming the two of them were
kindred spirits. For many years he had longed to meet the famous
Khotso, albeit he believed they often came together in thought.
Amigo then declared he was glad I had come, adding that my
friendship with Khotso had linked us together as well. Proffering a hand of welcome (the left one I noticed) he led me towards the lamp and gave me a stool to sit on.

During the following four days I sat with old Amigo beside
the smoky lamp, absorbing every word he spoke and fanning
away the stenchy heat that throbbed within the tiny shack.
Amigo was in many ways a puzzling old man and, in the way he
dealt with some of his customers, a source of bewilderment.
Sometimes gushing, sometimes quarrelsome and even rude, no
one seemed really to know what to make of him. He was short
and bony and always drenched in sweat that trickled in little
furrows from beneath a turban of soiled green towelling that
embraced his head. He lived the life of a recluse, no family, no
friends, no home except, of course, his beloved shop from which
he was apparently never seen to venture.

During the first two days together our discussions were confined largely to herbalism, and I was able to compare his stocks
of indigenous medicines with those normally kept by the practitioners in the interior of Southern Africa. Because of the ecologi-
cal differences between the drier regions in the west on the one
hand and the luxuriant east on the other, it was not surprising
that I should find several items I could not identify. So I asked
Amigo, somewhat naively now that I think of it, how many
varieties of medicines he had.

He replied facetiously that he only had ten fingers and ten
toes to count on, and had therefore never bothered to check.
There were many, however, as many as the flies on a Ronga
donkey's back, but considerably more useful to the Ronga than
either donkeys or flies.

'But,' added Amigo, becoming serious now, 'I have two main
kinds of medicine—the kind for the body and the kind for the
mind.'

He then explained that medicines for the body were plentiful
and of infinite variety. For example he had an analgesic made
from six different barks and a laxative prepared from five roots
and three bulbs. He also made blood-purifying tonics from
leaves, fruits and berries, which he ground together and boiled.
From the milky sap of the local euphorbia he made an ointment
for drawing boils, treating festering sores and even snake-bites.

But troubles of the mind, Amigo said, could only be cured
by the mind, for this was the mental winnowing basket which
sorted the chaff of fancy from the wheat of reality.

He told me of a patient who had been to see him the previous
week, a young dustman who sought to avenge a thrashing
he had received at the hands of a thug almost twice his size.
On arrival at Amigo's shack, the dustman had been full
of fear, knowing he could not hope to succeed unless fortified
with magical medicine. So the old herbalist had mixed him a
special potion studiously selecting ingredients for conditioning
the dustman's mind into positive action: a scraping of monkey
fat to give him guile; cobra fat for striking power; ground-up

Some of the indigenous medicinal herbs, bulbs,
bark and roots used by herbalists.

tortoise shell to ward off blows, and chameleon skin to make him elusive. To these he added antelope tendon for agility, lion fat for strength, mongoose liver for courage and rhinoceros horn for stamina. Sprinkled with powdered herbs, the ingredients were then thoroughly stirred, boiled and finally swallowed by the patient in a single gulp. The dustman soon believed that his body had been so fortified with the many qualities he had previously lacked that he was at last invincible. His fears vanished and he became suddenly obsessed with an urge to come to grips with the thug. Paying Amigo two hundred escudos, he declared he had never felt better.

'And the medicine worked,' chuckled Amigo, 'because two days later the thug turned up, battered and bruised, and I sold him the identical mixture the dustman had got.'

Looking around the shop with Amigo, I was amazed to learn that his 'medicines of the mind' were as much in demand as the large variety of herbs, roots, barks and leaves he dispensed for bodily aches and disorders. He sold hawk, vulture or eagle fat to elderly or lethargic patients about to embark on lengthy journeys, owl flesh or viscera to patients seeking to see better after dark, and crocodile liver to swamp-dwellers who sought to be immunized against attack by these fearsome creatures. He had a wide selection of lucky charms and amulets as well as talismanic figures carved from wood. Daubed with flamingo fat, these were bought for attaching to hut roofs, as a precaution against lightning. In addition there were Amigo's 'magical' divinatory bones, which I noticed he had occasion to consult on an average of five times a day at the request of patients, and in return for money.

The Magical Bones

Divination through the medium of the so-called magical bones is widely practised in Southern Africa, and its functions are manifold. It serves as a means of prediction, diagnosis and prognosis in cases of illness and general misfortune. It is used for making contact with the spirit world, and often for exorcizing evil influences. It is a demanding occupation, requiring not only a genuine sensitivity to psychic matters but also insight into the whims, inadequacies, frustrations and aspirations of humankind. It expects of its practitioners the qualities of patience, tolerance and understanding, as well as a facility for enduring the jibes of sceptics with an air of unconcern. For these reasons aspirant diviners are required to undergo three years of strict apprenticeship under the critical eye of a proven mentor. Bone-throwing is therefore an occupation which is seldom undertaken halfheartedly and has no place for charlatans.

A set of divinatory bones, like the one used by Amigo and scores of other diviners I know, consists of more than the collection of animal astragalus and phalange bones which most people imagine. Indeed, depending on such factors as locality, tradition and the personal preferences and psychic gifts of the practitioner himself, it may also include pips, carved sticks, pebbles, claws, beaks, teeth, hoof-tips and even coins, dice, marbles and fragments of coloured glass. Although techniques in throwing differ little from diviner to diviner, interpretations may vary according to the training received and, more especially, the practitioner's sensitivity to spiritual matters. So, when the bones are cast on a patient's behalf, it is not so much the visible patterns they make that count, as the 'messages' they project clairvoyantly or clairaudiently into the diviner's mind.

Of the multiplicity of items to be found in a diviner's set, the most important are the astragalus and phalange bones. These are usually selected in pairs to denote males and females of all

ages and walks of life—fathers, mothers, brothers, sisters, uncles, aunts, kings, queens, councillors, commoners, psychics, herbalists, transgressors and, of course, the ancestral spirits. Together with the other items, these bones may also point to material possessions, to moods and to events past, present and impending.

Looking through Amigo's divinatory set I found the bones of many different animals: *lion*, meaning among other things the head of the nation, authority, the tribal court of justice and ritual; *hyena*, denoting the councillors of the tribe, all 'yes-men' and sycophants who seek the company of their superiors, in much the same way as the hyena follows the lion from kill to kill; meaning also impending bewitchment, duplicity, intrigue and hypocrisy; *antbear*, pointing to death, burial and mourning; as an elusive creature which dwells underground in darkness, the antbear's bones also represent the ancestral world; *baboon*, a gregarious animal, therefore signifying the family unit, kraals, huts and domestic affairs; *monkey*, meaning cunning, deceit, all transactions requiring speedy action and guile; *goat*, a domestic animal referring to all members of the patient's family, and indeed the patient himself.

Among the antelopes, *kudu*, among other things, denotes vigilance; *springbok*, speed, pursuit, escape; *duiker* (a small South African antelope), a journey, travellers, partings and destinations; *steenbok*, gentleness, humility, shyness, kindness and favours done and received. Finally, *leopard* means regality, dignity, riches and longevity; and *bush pig*, herbalists, diviners, medicine, cure and convalescence.

Connotations for objects other than bones are: *sea shells*, the army, warriors, war, victory, defeat, heroism, cowardice, weapons, and in the case of females, fertility, fidelity and promiscuity; *tortoise shells*, events good or bad, luck and happiness; *crocodile stomach-stones*, defilement, treachery, doom, death, bewitchment and sorcery; *marulla pips*, health, disease, medicine, the seasons and crops; *ox-hoof tips*, the herds, prosperity, status; and, finally, *claws* or *beaks* which show direction.

A practitioner's interpretation of the divinatory bones depends on the positions into which the objects fall in relation to each other. Another important factor is whether they settle in a convex or 'mobile' position, a concave or 'immobile' position, or on their sides.

As a preliminary to inducing the bones into prompt response, the diviner may make use of hallowed home-brewed beer, hallowed water or even salt, snuff, ash and herbs. Almost without exception he will call upon the spirit world for guidance, either audibly for the patient to hear, or inwardly in private prayer. He may not always follow the same procedure, for much depends on how he is moved from within. I noticed that Amigo chose sometimes to sing, sometimes to beat out a rhythm on a sacred

An agglomeration of 'magical'
ingredients used by exorcizers
—sharks' teeth, animal and bird
bones, skulls, bulbs, hair,
quills, bark, horns,
mongoose and
hedgehog flesh.

A diviner named Khiba in action. Utensils and indigenous medicines being arranged on skins.

Hallowed water sprinkled with a wildebeest tail switch.

Final touches to the arrangement of the medicines.

Diviner takes a draught of hallowed water.

She places divinatory bones in palm of left hand.

The diviner breathes her own spirit into the bones.

Divinatory bones cupped in both hands.

Now she casts the bones on to the zebra skin.

Studying the positions into which the items have fallen.

A detailed description requiring the use of a pointer.

The interpretation begins.

The summing up and final predictions.

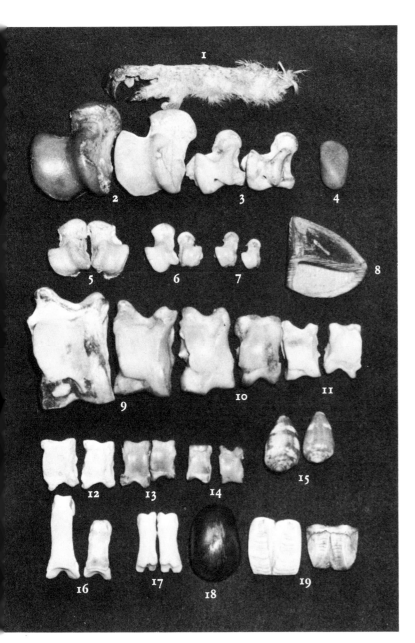

Divinatory 'bones', the items in pairs representing males and females; 1, owl's foot; 2, lion; 3, hyena; 4, crocodile stomach stone; 5, antbear; 6, baboon; 7, monkey; 8, oxhoof; 9, kudu; 10, bush pig; 11, springbok; 12, goat; 13, duiker; 14, steenbok; 15, oliva shells; 16, lion; 17, leopard; 18, *marulla* pip; 19, tortoise shell.

drum and sometimes to seek the mood he required by going into trance.

The Marsh-Dwellers of Djongaland

After four days with Amigo I had to return to Johannesburg but promised to keep in touch with him by post. As he was illiterate he would arrange for a local teacher to read my letters to him. He made me promise to come back soon, and I told him I would do so the moment I had completed my biography of King Dingane.

Our next meeting took place in December 1963, in the same shack, beside the same grimy paraffin lamp and in the same stenchy atmosphere. Having been commissioned meanwhile to write a book on the psychic and spiritual beliefs of African peoples both tribal and urban, I had hoped to photograph him in action with the divinatory bones. But Amigo would permit me to take no more than his portrait. He had been warned by his spirit mentor, he said, never to reveal his skills beyond the walls of his herbalist shop. If he should make even this one exception, he feared he might be deprived of his psychic powers.

The main purpose, however, for this second study trip to Mozambique was to open the way for researches I intended conducting among the Tsonga tribes to the north of Lourenço Marques. So after remaining with Amigo for a short while I spent a few days in the outlying tribal districts, noting the skill with which the Ronga built their rondavel huts and outdoor kitchens from poles, daub and thatch, and taking photographs of their outdoor pantries and potteries. I also noted the foods they prepared from groundnuts, wild spinach and the many indigenous fruits and berries they collected, in the lush, sub-tropical surrounding countryside.

A week later I headed northwards, spending a day in the Palmeira district, ninety kilometres from Lourenço Marques. I then moved on past Lake Chudi to Joao Belo and slightly westwards into the marshy territory of the Djonga tribe. It was among these people that I came to the kraal of Antonio Guye. A young, fuzzy-haired fellow with laughing eyes and sparkling teeth, he lived with his wife, his two children, his goats, pigs and poultry on an island in the marshes no bigger than a tennis court.

The countryside around Antonio's island, although hilly in parts, is mostly flat and carpeted with lilac-tinted water lily, bulrush and hyacinth. Through it winds the Limpopo river, and popping up everywhere high above the marshes are other islands similar to the one where Antonio lived. In December the marshes seethe in the summer sun, and the air is still and steamy. Day and

Ronga woman sorting
groundnuts.

Ronga potter with a newly-made
earthen pot.

One of the many kraals built on tiny islands in
the marshes of Djongaland, Mozambique.

A Djonga fisherman's kraal
fronted with marsh
waters.

Djonga woman
with pot of
sorghum beer.

night they resound to an orchestration of frog and insect song.

When I met Antonio for the first time, I found him fishing knee deep in water below the huts, a rod gripped firmly in his muddy hands. I had barely greeted him when a barbel snatched up his bait. He yelled with delight, tugging at his line, and then bringing the whiskered creature skidding towards us over the water and through the sludge. No sooner had he unhooked it than he held it high for me to see, and with a toothy grin he cried: 'White man, you have brought me luck!'

Thus began our happy friendship, one that was to grow with the years, but to end abruptly in 1967, when misfortune struck Antonio's island.

After our chance meeting in the marshes Antonio and I were together on six of the ten days I worked in Djonga territory. We travelled round the shallow waters in his little homemade canoe, calling on the islands and meeting his friends. Then one morning he paddled me towards the sea. Entering the Limpopo river we came upon an immense circle of tribesmen netting shrimps, lobsters, crayfish, crabs and a miscellany of fish that the tides had fed into the river mouth. Along the edge of the lagoon parties of men were at work with conical plunging-baskets, not unlike those used in Ovamboland, and here and there we could see women and children scaling and cleaning and salting mullet, to be taken home for drying.

Antonio and his family lived in two square huts each about five metres across and made of reed and clay. Close by was a goat pen, a pig sty and two small runs for fowls and Muscovy ducks. Six umbrella-shaped acacia trees shaded the huts from the punishing sun. At the foot of the island by the edge of the marshes were patches of maize, millet, sweet cane, sweet potato, groundnuts and beans. Beneath the farthest acacia were two cairns which marked the graves of Antonio's parents. His livestock included a sow and five piglets (the boar had recently died from the sting of a cobra), three goats and about fifteen fowls and ducks whose purpose, Antonio assured me facetiously, was not only to provide the family with eggs, but also to give marauding otters and iguana chickens to gorge. Long rows of dehydrated barbel had been strung between the branches of the trees. Beside the huts, spread out on woven mats to dry, were shrimps and fishes and wedges of turtle flesh. The smell of the little island was the smell of fish, and of decaying water weed rising from the marshes below. Antonio and the neighbouring islanders lived the humdrum life of impoverished fisherfolk, and yet when the time came to leave them and go deeper into the marshes I knew I would return one day to this delightful spot just west of Joao Belo.

Four years were to pass before I travelled again to Mozambique. I spent a day with Antonio at Xipamanine, and then headed northwards, skirting Joao Belo and continuing along the coast through the forest regions of Chidenguele and Inharrime. Farther up I crossed the swampy flats to the left of Lake Poelela, and then finally came to the Bay of Inhambane. I had hoped to go about twenty kilometres inland from the bay, but due to the recent rains the tracks had become impassable and the surroundings too muddy to cover either by truck or on foot. The more distant kraals were therefore inaccessible. So I remained in Inhambane for a week, going out each day to the local villages, which I found tucked away in dense plantations of coconut palm. I made a photographic record of their outstanding craftsmanship, the spoons, ladles, bowls, head-rests and snuffboxes they carved from *nkuhla* wood. Also the weird designs they engraved on to scoops and mugs made of coconut shell.

Particularly attractive were the grotesque animal and human figures they cut into walking sticks and handles of spoons and stirrers. These were the finest I had seen in Southern Africa. Most impressive of all were long chains they had cut from the trunks of trees, the links perfectly symmetrical and each end of the chain adorned with carvings of human, bird or animal heads.

I moved southwards from Inhambane towards Lake Poelela and into the territory of the Chopi clan. Like the Djonga, the Chopi are fisherfolk, but they are also in many ways the most colourful people of southern Mozambique. They are, for example, the most gifted musicians south of the Zambezi river, their homemade instruments ranging from modest flutes to drums and xylophones, large and small. Another point worthy of mention is that although age-old tribal tradition has long been on the wane in Southern Africa, the Chopi have not entirely abandoned the *hleta* practice, that is, filing their teeth into points.

The Marshes in Flood

From Chopi territory I returned to Joao Belo and thence to Antonio's island. On arrival I was amazed at the transformation the place had undergone since my visit four years before. The beautiful island I had once known had now been burnt dry in the wake of a scorching drought. The Limpopo waters were reduced to a trickle, the marshes to a crusty wasteland, and the water lilies had vanished. Meeting Antonio on the island in the shade of the acacia trees, it suddenly occurred to me that he had rebuilt his huts, and where two of the acacia trees had stood before there were now two splintered stumps. I learned from Antonio that lightning had struck his kraal during the previous summer, setting his huts alight, destroying his goats, pigs and poultry and snapping the trees into little pieces.

So he had rebuilt the huts and had himself, his family and the island cleansed by an exorcizer. Believing the lightning had been

One of the scores of Tsonga villages tucked
away in coconut plantations south of Inhambane.

Goatherds grazing their charges in the marshes
near Joao Belo.

sent by a sorcerer, he had consulted a diviner and procured from him the necessary medicines and amulets to protect the island from further misfortune.

Ever since that tragic day Antonio said, his mind had been plagued with doubts and fears. What made him really unhappy was the fact that some marsh-dwellers believed his island was still defiled, and therefore the cause of the prevailing drought.

After an hour I took leave of Antonio, promising to call again in the following year, when I returned to continue my studies in the north.

In the early summer of 1967 a cyclone swept across Mozambique from the Indian Ocean, followed by a deluge of rain that lasted for over a fortnight. I set out for Lourenço Marques in mid-December, and returning to Joao Belo hastened to Antonio's kraal. But it had disappeared. The island was bare like an inverted basin and its slopes deep in decaying debris. The marshes, I was told by a Djonga fisherman, had been lashed by rains, and the huts, trees and canoes scattered by blasting winds. The islanders had been panic-stricken, and as walls of floodwater came rolling in from the broken banks of the river, they had started to flee.

As if the storm and the floods were not cause enough for terror, the rising waters had brought in their flow crocodiles, snakes and scorpions from out of the sedges of the Limpopo river. Struggling to reach land, they had made for the islands, which soon became nests of lethal life. Fortunately the majority of the marsh-dwellers had already taken to their boats and headed for the hills, but some were stranded and had climbed into tree tops. Below them, drifting slowly to the sea, was a writhing mass of uprooted trees and animal carcasses and a vast assortment of flotsam and jetsam.

By the time I arrived in the area the floods had subsided, and an eerie quiet hung over the marshes. I was eager to move on to the north, but was delayed by an urge to locate Antonio. I found him far sooner than I had expected. Told by goat-herds he had been picked up injured during the storm by a Portuguese rescue launch, I decided to make enquiries at Joao Belo. Questioning Africans in the streets I was surprised to discover that they all seemed to know him.

'You're looking for the bewitched one that the lightning struck,' one of them said. 'Until last week he was walking up and down the streets on crutches, begging for food. He is being looked after now by a Portuguese shopkeeper. I will take you to him.'

I was brought to Antonio in a disused garage in the yard of a trading store. His clothes were tattered, his hair tousled and his face a study of abject despair. In former times it had been his custom to hail my arrival with a flourish of greetings and bles-

sings and happy laughter. Now he could barely muster a smile, and his voice was thin and croaky.

I told him how shocked I had been to find his kraal destroyed. I was delighted to find him alive, I said, and recovering from his recent injuries. Soon he would be strong enough to build new huts and make new gardens. For several minutes Antonio gazed impassively at the floor. He seemed not to have heard my words. Eventually lifting his face he looked at me with pleading eyes.

'There is nothing more to do,' he said, 'because soon I must die!'

'No Antonio,' I protested, 'you are young and strong and have many years to live. Don't talk to me of dying.'

'Soon I must die,' he cried impulsively.

'But why?' I asked.

'Because I am cursed to die,' he replied, sobbing now. 'Can't you see I want to die?'

Antonio then told me he would never return to the marshes. Knowing he was doomed, he had already sent his wife and children to relatives in Canicado, an inland village on the Limpopo river.

'Antonio,' I ventured, 'I have a wonderful plan. Instead of going straight away to the tribes in the north, I will stay a while in Joao Belo, and take you to see Amigo, the diviner near Lourenço Marques. He will remove the curse you speak of.'

'No! No!' he rasped, 'I don't want to see Amigo. There are plenty of diviners among my own people, the Djonga, and I don't want to see them either. You must leave me here in Joao Belo, and when you return from the north, perhaps we can talk again.'

There was nothing I could do. Antonio's inner entanglement could be unravelled only by Antonio himself. So I left him in the gloom of the garage, steeped in the gloom of his thoughts. He scarcely lifted his eyes to say farewell.

Three weeks later when I called by at Joao Belo on my way home from the north, I returned to the Portuguese trading store, hoping to find Antonio in a happier frame of mind. But he was not there. At the disused garage I found an old man smoking a pipe in the shade of a nearby shrub.

'You're looking for Antonio?' he queried.

'Yes,' I replied.

'He is dead and buried,' he said. Then, pointing to the roof of the garage with the stem of his pipe, he continued: 'Antonio knew he had to die, so about three weeks ago he hanged himself from one of the rafters up there.'

Pausing to gather my thoughts I could hear the ring of Antonio's laughter within me. And my thoughts were of the days we had spent happily together in the marshes near Joao Belo.

And what of Amigo? Our friendship continues to thrive. His shack has hardly changed in all the years I have known him, except that it has become more cluttered now, and perhaps the smell a little stronger. I am told he has recently entered his dotage, but that his patients have multiplied in direct proportion to his mounting eccentricities. The people of Xipamanine say he can never die, for even in death his spirit will continue to live with them. That is how much they love old Victor Hugo Makumbuyo, diviner, herbalist and exorcizer, that shrivelled old hermit whom everyone calls Amigo.

Swaziland

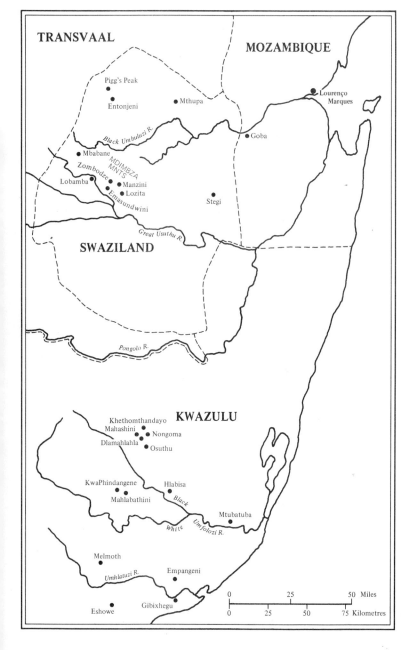

King Sobhuza II

South-west of Mozambique, beyond the Lubombo mountains, lies the kingdom of Swaziland, a pinch of territory no more than one hundred and ninety kilometres long and a hundred wide. A land so fair it must have been triple-touched with nature's magic wand; a land of the proverbial milk and honey, of mountains, woodlands, valleys, streams and waterfalls. A land blessed with abundant rains, lush grasslands and fertile soil. So small a gem, and yet so bright its sparkle.

The Swazi are a small nation ruled by the elderly King Sobhuza II. I met this wise and revered monarch in 1955 at Emasundwini—Place of the Isundu Palm—a majestic, rambling house occupied in colonial days by a succession of British resident commissioners. It was an event I have cherished over the years, for of all the leading personages in Southern Africa few are as widely known, deeply respected and loved as this bearded Ingwenyama or Lion, as he is called, the mystical King Sobhuza. Other meetings were to follow, each of which I regarded as an important milestone in my career as a student of African peoples.

Looking back over the years, I can see him now simply but impeccably dressed in Swazi regalia: a single string of beads around his neck, a red floral print cloth across the chest, a purple loin cloth, and in his long greying hair a scarlet wing-feather of the purple-crested loerie bird. I can see him too, on a different occasion, in top hat, tails, pin-stripe trousers and glittering shoes, spruced to welcome visiting Western dignitaries to his domain. Finally I see him at the head of his befurred and befeathered regiments, on a day of national ritual, his head adorned with a lofty crown of assorted plumes, his chest crossed with beads, and around his waist a kilt of skins. No matter what the occasion I have seen him always as a powerful yet humble man, in many ways the most regal figure in tribal Southern Africa.

Harking back on my long association with the Swazi nation, a second figure enters my mind. He is Prince Makhungu (the Mist) Dlamini, son of Sobhuza II, and for many years my guide and informant in Swaziland. It was he who named me Vulindlela, Opener of the Road, at a small ceremony attended by Swazi dignitaries in 1955. At that time the prince and I had spent a fortnight together in the lowlands of the Hhohho district, visiting kraals, interviewing chiefs, councillors and medicine men, and talking ceaselessly about Swazi beliefs and customs. Indeed it was also he who first introduced me to his illustrious father, and then soon afterwards to the reigning Queen Mother of the nation—Nukwase Nxumalo Ndwandwa—known to the Swazi as Indlovukati or She-Elephant.

Of the many royal and military kraals dotted over Sobhuza

Swazi married woman.

Swazi patriarch.

Swazi kraalhead of the lowveld regions.

Prince Makhungu Dlamini.

II's kingdom, the largest and most important is the queen mother's capital, Lobamba. It is here that she resides, surrounded by a swarm of devoted followers, like a human queen bee of a human hive. Dominating the whole of Lobamba is an immense palisade cattlefold, a venue of religious ceremony as sacred to the Swazi nation as St Peter's cathedral is to Italians or St Paul's to Englishmen. To the left and right of the cattlefold, facing westwards, are the military barracks, comprising hundreds of huts occupied by regiments appointed to keep guard over the queen and her people. A little farther on, separated from these huts by an open space, and cut off from the rest of Lobamba by tall, circular hedges made of reed, is the *indlunkulu*, or queen mother's section, and beside it the *sigodlo* or seraglio, where the king's more senior wives are housed. Next come the retainers' quarters, a multiplicity of rondavel homes built side by side in the form of a mammoth crescent, the tips converging on to the barracks, and the bulge making a bulwark of humanity, mortar and reed. Nowhere in Southern Africa are huts as magnificently built and beautifully kept as they are at Lobamba. Most impressive of all are the dome-shaped, beehive huts, for they conform to the highest standards of Swazi workmanship in wood and thatch. The rondavel homes are not nearly as attractive. They are nonetheless neatly made and neatly kept, and screened like most others in Lobamba with reed.

Whilst visiting the Swazi in July 1955, I asked Prince Makhungu to explain to me the roles played by the king, on the one hand, and the queen mother on the other in the affairs of the nation.

'To begin with my father, King Sobhuza II,' he had said 'one must realize that he is more than just a ruler. In the eyes of the Swazi he stands for everything that is good, and by his example are the standards of behaviour and etiquette set throughout the land. He is held in such great esteem by the nation—commoners, the regiments, headmen, councillors, chiefs and princes alike—that he comes daily into our prayers. We have no greater wish than that he should always be healthy. For when we know he is well, then somehow we feel that all things are well. But should we hear he is ill, we all become concerned, not only for his health, feeling the suffering within ourselves, but also for the future of Swaziland. You see, the king means everything to us; his death would be seen as a disaster. In fact, this was exactly the feeling our forefathers had for the kings that reigned over them.

'The Swazi have not known what it means for a king to die since December, 1899, when my grandfather, King Bhunu, passed suddenly away,' Makhungu continued. 'At the best of times death can be a complicated matter, but when it comes to the death of a king, the whole nation, every single one of us, becomes involved.'

The Prince explained further that in centuries past when a king's health began to decline the Swazi were so overwhelmed with anxiety that they could speak of nothing else. So they made regular sacrifices to the spirit world, praying that his life should be spared and their sorrowing hearts restored to joy. And when the time came for a king to pass on to a higher life, the news was kept secret from everyone, all, that is, except members of the royal family, the royal councillors and the *tinsila* or blood brothers who had been his closest companions and confidants. The death of a king brought winter to the land even when it occurred in the summer. Burial did not take place immediately for, as the gloom of winter is followed by a glorious rebirth of leaf, blossom and seed, there could be no more appropriate time for a king's interment than in the spring when nature itself comes back to life.

The practice of delaying the burial of a monarch until the coming of spring is not exclusive to the Swazi nation. After the death of King Mzilikazi, founder of the Matabele dynasty in Rhodesia, for example, the corpse was kept in a special hut for three months. Although he had died early in September, at the beginning of spring, his burial was held back until November owing to the late arrival of the new season's rains. Only when the elders were satisfied that nature had been truly resurrected, did they announce the burial day. Conditions had to be perfect for the 'going home' of their beloved king.

In Swaziland the burial of a king has always drawn the nation in multitudes to the capital kraal. As part of the mourning the women shave their heads, turn their oxhide aprons back to front and remove top-notches from the beehive huts. Mourning lasts three years, and the nation as a whole is subjected to strict taboos and disciplines. On the appointed day the royal corpse is taken by handpicked bearers to the foot of Mdimbza, a sacred range that tumbles eastwards from Mbabane to Manzini. Flanked by the regiments, their shields held upside down, and followed by a procession of mourners chanting age-old dirges, it is handed over to members of the Gama clan, the custodians of the royal burial grounds who live on the slopes of Mdimbza. To this day only the Gama people know where the graves are situated. Even King Sobhuza is prohibited by ancient tribal law from visiting the sacred spot where he himself will be interred one day.

A fascinating aspect of my discussions with Prince Makhungu and other members of the Swazi royal house was the question of succession after the death of a Swazi king. This, according to my informants, had always been a complicated matter, leading to lengthy and often heated debate among the late king's blood brothers, the chiefs of clans, the royal councillors and the

Swazi platters and spoons.

She-Elephant's advisers. Since Swazi custom does not allow for automatic succession, the heir-apparent has had to be chosen from a large number of heirs-presumptive. Final selection has been determined not so much by the qualities and attributes of the successful candidate himself as by those of his royal mother. This is well illustrated in the case of the present king, Sobhuza II, for he was an infant in arms when proclaimed heir-apparent in 1899, and his mother the most distinguished and respected of the late King Bhunu's queens.

'It has always been the custom,' Prince Makhungu said, 'that the choice of the heir-apparent should be followed by a general announcement first to the queen mother, then to the children of the departed king and lastly to the nation as a whole. The king-to-be is called Umntwana, or child, even though he may already have reached maturity. His mother is known as UnaBomtwana, which simply means, the mother of the "child". On the day of the coronation this important woman becomes the Indlovukati, or She-Elephant, queen mother of the nation.'

In the twenty-one years before he became of age, and was crowned King of the Swazi, Sobhuza II's grandmother Queen Labotsibeni, assisted by her son Malunge, acted as regent of the nation. In the meantime the young Umntwana Sobhuza was being prepared by the royal elders for his impending role as Lion of the nation: he was given lessons in Swazi court procedure, etiquette and protocol; in Swazi law and justice, folk ways, religious belief and ritual; in day-to-day dealings with the more mundane aspects of Swazi life.

On reaching puberty he was sent to Swaziland's newly founded Zombodze National School, and at sixteen departed for the far-off Cape Colony to further his studies at the Ciskeian Loveday Institute. Thereafter he returned to his homeland, and was crowned Ingwenyama, the Lion, King of the Swazi, in 1921.

Although endowed with considerable power and innumerable prerogatives, Swazi kings have seldom been dictatorial. In theory they have had influence over every aspect of Swazi life, yet in actual practice they have been subject to strict controls. Major decisions, for example, can only be taken after consultation with a privy council or, depending on circumstances, with a general council called the *libandla*. On the rare occasions when a king has defied the advice of his councillors, he has been summoned by the She-Elephant, who as his mother, and mother of the nation, has the right to rap him over the proverbial knuckles. In any case tradition has always demanded the closest cooperation and the highest level of communication between the Lion and the She-Elephant in matters of national importance. As one of the She-Elephant's councillors once put it to me: the lion can

never roar too loudly lest its ears are deafened with the trumpeting of elephants.

Queen Mother Nukwase

It is not easy to arrange an interview with the She-Elephant, especially if one is a stranger, as indeed I was in 1955. After negotiating with her councillors, however, Prince Makhungu persuaded them to let me see her provided, of course, she herself agreed. So early one morning we were summoned to Lobamba. Arriving at the main gates we were met by a party of Swazi warriors bearing V-shaped battle-axes and fighting sticks. Headed by the commander in chief of Lobamba, Councillor Kopolo Shongwe, they were a fine body of men, immaculately dressed in tribal regalia. Shongwe came forward to greet us, and summoning two warriors to help me carry my camera equipment led us into the great royal kraal. We passed the king's seraglio to the right of the main gates, paused to inspect a huge beehive hut laden with cattle horns, and then moved on into the heart of the settlement. On either side of us were rows of smaller beehive huts, all screened with reed hedges. Then suddenly we came to a small bungalow among a cluster of huts. Ushered on to the verandah by Kopolo Shongwe, we were told to be seated on a goat skin laid out for us on the floor. We passed the following half hour in silence, and then Queen Nukwase appeared. I caught sight of her shuffling towards us across a yard between the huts. Several royal children ran up to greet her. A bevy of handmaidens who chanced to enter the yard at that moment came suddenly to a halt and stood before her in obeisance. Smiling gently she touched the little ones lovingly on the head, and greeted the girls with a friendly nod.

Queen Nukwase was far older than I had expected. She was about seventy-five, yet her face was surprisingly smooth and her eyes alert. Slightly stooped, she wore a light-blue blanket around her waist and a voluminous cowhide cloak which reached down to the ankles. As is the fashion among Swazi women, her hair was combed upwards into the shape of a dome, not unsimilar in appearance to an undersized busby. Around the base of the dome was a narrow band made of carved sticks and fronted with a pale-pink feather of the flamingo, Swaziland's bird of rain. Queen Nukwase wore few ornaments which, I reflected, was not uncommon among African women of very high rank: a short necklace of beads, seeds and porcupine quills, and around her wrists and ankles wooden amulets to match her headband. She was barefooted and carried neither fly switch nor staff as so many of the older people do.

Reaching the verandah the old She-Elephant first greeted

Kopolo Shongwe, then Prince Makhungu, and finally the rest of us. She then sank into a large chair draped with leopard skins, and in a soft voice asked Makhungu my name, and the purpose of my visit to Lobamba. Learning I had visited tribes in other parts of Southern Africa, had met their kings and chiefs, and had studied their customs and beliefs, her face lit up with curiosity. Learning too that I could speak her language she smiled, and as if to test my fluency asked me if I had met King Cyprian, Lion of the neighbouring Zulu nation. When I replied that I had been to see him a year before, she said she had heard he was a sickly man. This caused her sorrow, especially as he was still so very young. She had known his father, the late King Solomon, and had admired him, as indeed she had always admired the imposing line of Zulu kings before him—Shaka, Dingane, Mpande, Cetshwayo and Dinuzulu. It pleased her to think that the Swazi and Zulu nations were brothers in origin, and hoped that in time to come the Swazi and Zulu royal houses would grow closer together. Returning to King Cyprian, she said she had reason to believe that I would one day play a significant role in helping him back to health. This in turn would bind me in friendship with the Zulu nation until my dying day. Little did I know at the time that this prediction would soon come true.

We then chatted for over an hour about the customs and beliefs of the more distant peoples of Southern Africa, and eventually, when I could sense the queen was growing weary, I placed before her a selection of woodcuts, line drawings and photographs of Swazi kings, queens and other dignitaries, including herself, which I had recently unearthed in Johannesburg. These captured her interest, and she chuckled with child-like delight. With the aid of Makhungu and Shongwe she began pointing out friends and relatives, some of them long deceased, others like herself greatly changed in the passage of time and still others, infants and children, who were now in the prime of adulthood. Prince Makhungu told me later he had never seen the old She-Elephant quite so elated and talkative.

When in due course she decided she had had enough of us, she rose from the chair, bade us farewell, and then retraced her steps across the yard. Ten minutes later a messenger arrived with a request from the queen that I lend her the pictures. She would return them to me on the morrow.

Swazi Dignitaries

I remained three days at Lobamba making a detailed study of hut construction, weapons, foodstuffs, utensils and ceremonial regalia. In the gathering place beneath the trees I also talked with the Swazi elders, who had played leading roles in the *Incwala* or

First Fruits ceremony and other rituals performed periodically in the nearby cattlefold. In those days I had not yet had the opportunity of witnessing the *Incwala*, most sensational of all tribal events in Southern Africa. Now, Makhungu assured me, I would be welcome to attend, for, as he put it, my visit to the She-Elephant had 'opened the gates'. Three days later when I called on the She-Elephant to greet her before leaving Lobamba, I promised to return for the *Incwala* in six months' time.

As events turned out I was to wait not six months but six years before attending an *Incwala* ceremony. For my writing career had started to blossom, and I found myself either bound to my desk or deeply involved in archival or field research. During that period I wrote *Sandy Tracks* followed by three volumes entitled *The Peoples of South Africa*. I had also been commissioned to write the biography of the Matabele king, Mzilikazi, and this took me to the network of trails he and his conquering armies had trodden from KwaZulu through central South Africa, the northern reaches of the Kalahari Desert and finally Rhodesia. I did manage to call on the She-Elephant in July 1956, but commitments again prevented my attending the *Incwala* at the end of the year. Soon after my visit the old queen became seriously ill, and she died in January 1957. She was succeeded by Queen Zihlathi Nxumalo, one of the king's wives.

During the following year I returned to Swaziland accompanied by my son Harold and the German film-makers, Molli Franke and Wolf Kaiser. I had arranged with Prince Makhungu that he would act as our guide, but on arriving at his home found him indisposed and confined to bed. His place was taken by an influential Swazi councillor named Mamba. He took us into the bushy lowveld regions of Swaziland, where we visited Mthupa, royal kraal of Gija the short, stout and happy-go-lucky chief of the Mayiwane clan. We filmed Chief Gija's tribal court in session beneath the trees, his womenfolk brewing sorghum beer within a reed enclosure and squads of maidens gracefully dancing to the strains of a *ligubu*, a wooden bow strung with a single metal string, fitted at the top with a spherical gourd which resonates when the string is tapped with a twig.

From Chief Gija's kraal we headed for Entonjeni in the Pigg's Peak district, one of King Sobhuza's military kraals. We spent an hour in the barracks among the regiments, and then later two more hours watching the warriors as they went through a series of traditional military manoeuvres—charging, attacking, loping, swerving and parrying assegai thrusts with an imaginary foe; chanting, hissing and humming—all in view of our cameras.

The commander of the regiments at Entonjeni, Mabutana Mdluli, was a veteran warrior, enormously fat but as agile as a jackal cub. Leading the warriors in all this activity, his voice deep and sonorous like the bellow of a bull, he became a veritable

Young Swazi men enjoying the leisure that
comes with *mnganu* time.

fountain of sweat. And when the manoeuvres were over, and
the regiments had withdrawn to the shade of the trees close by,
he led us back to the barracks and brought us before the chieftain
in charge of Entonjeni, Majahane Dlamini. He was a short, thin,
friendly man. A prince of the Swazi royal house, he was said to
be King Sobhuza's 'eyes, ears and nose', a man of unquestionable
calibre whose responsibilities included superintending the king's
seraglio, and seeing to the rations not only of the warriors and
retainers of Entonjeni, but also of the resident dignitaries, their
wives and children.

On the following day we were taken by Mamba to Zombodze,
one of Swaziland's oldest and best-known royal kraals, situated
near the eastern extremity of the sacred Mdimbza range. The
head of Zombodze was the revered and aged Mandanda
Mthethwa, senior chief of Swaziland, whom the regent queen
mother, Labotsibeni, had appointed chief councillor of the
nation as far back as the 1920s. Wizened and greybearded, he met
us at the door of his beehive hut. He wore on his head the traditional symbol of Swazi aristocracy, a headring made of a mixture
of finely ground roots and beeswax. Chief Mandanda was the
epitome of Swazi regality, an excellent subject for Franke's
cameras and, of course, my own.

Originally the royal capital of the ancestral king, Mbandzeni,
Sobhuza II's grandfather, Zombodze has always been sacred to
the Swazi. It was similar in appearance to most other royal
kraals and, with the exception of Lobamba, by far the largest of

Chief Gija.

A councillor of Chief Gija's Mthupa royal kraal.

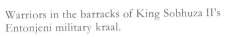
Warriors in the barracks of King Sobhuza II's
Entonjeni military kraal.

Reveille at Entonjeni military kraal.

Dawn patrol on the outskirts
of the Entonjeni.

Mabutana Mdluli, commander of the Entonjeni
regiments in 1957.

Chief Mandanda Mthethwa in 1957.

all. We took photographs of Chief Mandanda in various parts of his historic kraal, arriving at length at the cattlefold where we found three of his servants skinning a beast they had found dead in the veld. It was sunset when we left Zombodze bound for a camping sight on the Usuthu river. Next morning Franke and Kaiser declared they had seen enough of Swaziland's scenic beauty and its colourful people to convince them of its potential for filming. We returned to Johannesburg far sooner than I had expected.

'Ingwenya! Ingwenya! Crocodile! Crocodile!'

In February 1959 I received a message from Prince Makhungu one morning that a young Swazi called Madliza Mathonsi had been attacked and savaged by a crocodile at the Nogwane drift, in the Black Umbuluzi river. Collecting my cameras I hurried off to Swaziland, my curiosity prodded by the fact that a six-year-old girl had suffered a similar fate, in the very same drift, three years before, and that the incident had been attributed to witchcraft. Even more intriguing, according to Makhungu, was that the newest victim had been rescued by the girl's father, Amos Magagula. I reached the banks of the river on a Tuesday afternoon, and after a brief search among kraals in the neighbourhood came upon Amos's place. I found him together with his wife, Makhumalo, and three of their children in the shade of a *marulla* tree. Tall and sturdily built, he was sharpening a plough share with a file, a stumpy pipe wedged in the corner of his mouth. He rose to greet me, proffering a huge, fleshy hand, and called on a child to draw up a stool for me to sit on beside him. When I told him why I had come he seemed taken aback, then shook his head rather forlornly.

Amos Magagula (right) in the dreaded drift
where his daughter and neighbour were savaged
by crocodiles.

'This crocodile attack has been bad for all of us,' he said. 'First it was my daughter, Busisizwe, and now it has been Madliza Mathonsi's turn. There are unfriendly people in these parts who have been using black magic to drive us out of the area, Madliza's family and mine. What better way could there be than to send these monsters to kill us?'

'But why should they have wanted to get rid of you,' I asked. 'What have you done to them?'

'Nothing,' he replied. 'It is only because we are strangers here from the other side of the river. It is not everyone that trusts a stranger, particularly when there are complaints that land for planting and grazing is scarce in the district. We were threatened and warned to go back to the place we had come from, but we refused because these peoples' very own chief, who is now our chief, gave us permission to live here.'

'And so?' I prompted.

'And so somebody first bewitched my family, and then afterwards the young man, Madliza. As you know he was attacked by a crocodile last week, at the same spot where our little girl, Busisizwe, was almost killed. Just two months ago Madliza was told that if he wished to remain alive he must move back over the river and take his wife, his child and his animals with him. He was also told to burn down his hut and cattlefold before he left.'

'Tell me about Busisizwe,' I ventured, 'tell me exactly what happened to her.'

'It was exactly three years ago,' began Amos, 'on a day as hot as this one, when Busisizwe and her smaller sister, Shokozile, went down to the river to play in the sands. They were naughty to go without telling their mother. At the time she was patching clothes in the shade of this very tree whose shade we are sharing now. But you know how forgetful children can be when their minds are dancing with thoughts of play. Of course they knew there were crocodiles in the river, which makes me wonder even now what influence it was that enticed them there.

'Anyhow, as I was saying, my wife was quietly sewing here, while I myself was away in the bush searching for an ox that had strayed. All of a sudden she heard a scream, then more and more screams, and jumping to her feet she saw herdboys running away in all directions, and they were crying "*Ingwenya! Ingwenya!* —Crocodile! Crocodile!" And although by then many voices were shouting and the dogs were barking, she could hear someone cry "Busisizwe!", and she knew, as if seeing with her own two eyes, that our daughter had been taken by a crocodile.

'So she ran like a hare across the lands, through the trees, along the banks of the river, and then on to the sands where she saw our child, her right leg deep in the crocodile's throat, being dragged into the water. It was like watching a cat with a mouse in its mouth, my wife told me afterwards, except that this was her very own child, and the monster more powerful and dangerous than a whole hut full of vicious cats.

'My wife kept running, her strides growing longer and faster, and she was weeping and screaming "Yo-yo! Yo-yo!", as mothers do when something is seriously wrong. She grabbed hold of Busisizwe's arm and started pulling, pulling, pulling, and shouting for help, and calling out loudly for the Great Creator to save our child.

'She is not a big woman, as you can see,' continued Amos, turning to his wife, 'but she has become strong like an ox after working all these years in the fields. Slowly, slowly, little by little, the crocodile moved backwards into the water taking Busisizwe with it. And all the time my wife kept holding on to her arm, sliding and slipping and stumbling over the sands.

'Then suddenly something snapped and our daughter was free! But oh, what a sight remained for the mother to behold— Busisizwe's leg had been torn clean off, and that filth of a thing was swimming away with the torn-off part between its jaws.

'By this time people were rushing down to the river from all directions, and I myself was also running, because a herdboy had brought me the news in the bush. And when I reached my wife and Busisizwe, I could not see them at first, because of the crowd that had gathered around them. The women were waving their arms, crying "Yo! Yo!", and the men just stood there in silence, shaking their heads. I thought my daughter was dead. Then pushing my way through the crowd I came to her side. She was soaked in blood. Then I noticed that someone had strapped what remained of her leg with a thong, to stop the stream of life from pouring out. I picked her up in my arms, and carried her back to the hut. Soon afterwards a white man arrived in a truck and drove us to the hospital in Manzini.

'Everything had happened so suddenly, and everything was so very horrible, that I kept on saying to myself "Amos, perhaps you are dreaming". But no, it was all too real for a dream, and I could distinctly hear people talking of the sorcery that some enemy had brought upon me.'

'And do you still believe that you and your family were bewitched?' I asked.

'Of course I do,' cried Amos.

'But how can you really be sure?' I added, leading him on.

'Because it's something that no right-minded man would doubt,' he said, 'and no one in these parts would tell you otherwise.'

'What of Busisizwe?' I continued, 'is there not more to be told?'

'Plenty more,' he grinned, 'because wonderful things have since happened to our little girl. When once her leg had healed, she was taken to Johannesburg, fitted with a metal leg and taught to walk all over again. She is back in Swaziland now and goes to school in Mbabane.'

'But what of the sorcerer's curse?' I asked, 'what about that?'

'We got rid of it,' he said, 'and I'll tell you how. The day after the crocodile struck (or it might even have been the same day) I was visited by a white man who lives here in the bush and can shoot with a rifle as no other man can shoot. "Amos," he said to me, "we must kill that crocodile, for otherwise it will keep on attacking people who go down to the river." And then he asked me if I had a dog. So I showed him this big one which now lies asleep at our feet.

'Now, the white man got me to take my dog to the river, put a chain around its neck, and enter the shallow waters. He was sitting on a boulder near by, and we arranged that if the crocodile appeared again he would shoot it before it reached me. The idea of the dog was to feed it to the crocodile if for some reason the bullets failed. It was far better for the dog to be killed, the white man had said, than for me to die who had a wife and children to support.

'We were not long in the river, the dog and I, when, Oh God! there was a splash as if a log of wood had fallen into the water. The crocodile was coming! Yes, I could see it coming swiftly towards us, and my heart was beating, "Du-du!", just like the beat of a drum.

'To make things worse for me my dog, realizing that death was approaching, began struggling on the chain, splashing and yelping and even snarling at me, and I said to myself, "why does the white man not shoot?"

'Just at that moment he fired, again and again, and I could hear the bullets go into the crocodile's body. He kept on firing, and I, with the dog still tugging and struggling at the end of the

A herd of cattle drink languidly in the Black
Umbuluzi river. At this spot little Busisizwe's
leg was retrieved from the crocodile's stomach.

chain, made a dash for the bank, stumbling and shivering and believing the crocodile was about to get me.

'When I was safe on the sands and turned around, the first thing I saw was the monster lashing the water with its mighty tail, its big white stomach looking upwards and its stumpy legs and long-clawed feet pointing up to the heavens. It was dying, and I myself was laughing with joy. "We've got him," the white man cried out to me, and I shouted back: "Yes, we've got him, and now we'll see if it's the one that took Busisizwe's leg."

'Below the drift a mix-up of boulders and stones and fallen trees stick out of the water, so we waited there for the river to bring us the crocodile's body. It was huge. Its teeth like the spikes of a harrow, and its long mouth mocking us with the smile of the devil. With the help of eight of my neighbours we pulled the monster out of the water, cut open its stomach, and there in the depths of its bowels were the broken-up bones of Busisizwe's leg and parts of her feet. It was ugly to see and uglier to smell, but good to know we had killed the one we had wanted to kill.

'We who have lived for years on either side of the Umbuluzi river have seen quite a number of children caught by crocodiles. Only three I know of have managed to escape from those powerful jaws, and of these, two were eventually to die from poison left by the crocodile's filthy teeth in their wounds. Busisizwe's quick recovery, therefore, made her quickly known in most parts of Swaziland, and soon it was being said that the spirits had special plans for her, and would give her powers that few people possess. Who are we to say why this should have befallen us? Far better it is to know that just as the warmth of summer comes after the cold of winter, so sorrow gives birth to happiness. You see, shortly after that dreadful day things started to go better for us, and the fear of sorcery has left our minds.'

'And Madliza?' I asked.

'He was also bewitched,' Amos replied, 'but I hope he will return to us here in Nogwane as a new man, and with a life of good fortune before him.'

My chat with Amos made me all the more determined to meet Madliza Mathonsi, whose encounter with a crocodile five days before had brought me to Swaziland. I therefore headed for Manzini where I located him in the Nazarene hospital, his body bandaged from knees to neck, his right arm slung across his chest. From the little I could see of his plaster-patched face he looked no older than twenty-five. He was a frail little fellow, which made me all the more eager to record his story of the struggle he had had with the crocodile. I told him I had visited Amos, the one who had come to his rescue in the Nogwane drift. Would he tell me what had happened, I asked, assuring him there was no urgency. I could return in a few days' time, or even a week, or whenever he felt equal to the task. To my surprise he said he would be glad to talk with me now. Having been saved from death, he added, the joy in his heart outweighed the pains in his body, and his tongue was eager to tell.

'I came as a stranger to Nogwane two years ago,' Madliza began, 'and because I was new as Amos had been, and because it was said the grazing was scarce and that land for planting was even scarcer, I was warned to leave before someone tried to bewitch me. But I refused to go. You see, I was not unduly troubled. I had brought protective medicines to place in my hut and cattlefold, and had special amulets made for myself, my wife and my child. For a while we lived happily in our little kraal, but then last week I was crossing the river to visit a friend, and now you can see what happened to me.

'I was in the middle of the Nogwane drift, carrying an assegai as most of us do who know about crocodiles, when something inside me said "Today beware!" So, feeling a shiver go up my back I moved on faster, which is difficult in water that is up to the navel. Then looking to the right I saw a crocodile coming towards me. What could I do? I screamed "Ingwenya! Ingwenya!—Crocodile! Crocodile!" and in trying to run, I fell so that the water splashed over my head, and my eyes went blind.

'When I got back on to my feet and glanced over my shoulder the ingwenya was so close I could see its nostrils beside me. So I turned to face it, punching and pushing it away with my left hand, and digging the assegai into its head. But it came at me with snapping jaws, and catching hold of my punching arm started tearing it apart like a piece of rag. So I dug the assegai into its mouth and down, deep down into its throat. This made it grunt and release my arm, but then it came back at me and snatched at my stomach. Again the assegai went into its throat, and I kept digging and digging, screaming and digging and hoping it would leave me alone. But the crocodile was so big and heavy and vicious that it threw me over, and I could feel its claws cut into my face and chest.

'By now all fear had left me, for strangely I was longing to die. I just kept on digging with the assegai until my arm went numb and it fell from my hand. Then suddenly everything was quiet about me, and struggling to my feet I caught sight of the crocodile swimming away to the reeds.

'But then came the most frightening moment of all! There was no water around me! Just blood! There were also intestines floating beside me, and when suddenly I saw the hole in my stomach I screamed "Oh God they are mine!" My legs went soft beneath me, and the whole of Nogwane whirled around as if I was drunk from too much beer. Then Amos came! Amos my friend, and he picked me up in his arms, telling me all the time

Bush grandmother, Rakopo
district

Obies, the veteran Nama
hunter

that I would not die, and shouting with his loudest voice for help.

'I cannot remember what happened next, but I am told that Amos and a friend called Mahlalela pressed my intestines back into the hole, wrapped a cloth around my stomach and then carried me through the bush to a police camp three hours' walk from the drift. That's how I came to Manzini. And now I am waiting to go home to my wife and child.'

Madliza remained in hospital for two more weeks. I had meanwhile returned to Johannesburg, but learning of his arrival home I went back to the Nogwane drift to see him. Accompanied by Amos, I visited him at his kraal, where I found him seated on a goat skin in the shade of a hut, looking a little forlorn.

'Are you well, Madliza?' I asked.

'Not well,' he replied.

'His body is well,' inserted Amos, 'but what he means is that his mind is troubled and this makes him feel unwell. You see, he believes he is still bewitched, and must move away from Nogwane.'

'But is it not believed,' I continued, 'that by escaping from the crocodile you have gained special powers? This is what is said about Busisizwe you know.'

'No,' Madliza replied, 'no one has said these things of me, and in any case what would I do with special powers?'

'But how do you know you are still bewitched,' I persisted.

'Dreams, dreams!' cried Amos. 'He says his nights are haunted with dreams of dreadful things to come.'

In the hour that followed, as we sat talking together, I realized that as long as Madliza allowed his mind to juggle with forebodings, doubts and suspicions there was nothing either Amos or I could do for him. He now seemed half the man I had judged him to be when first I had met him at the hospital.

Two days later he, his wife and child disappeared from Nogwane.

'Madliza will have to travel many roads to find peace of mind,' Amos told me, 'and his is the most painful journey of all.'

First Fruits Ceremony

During the 1960s my studies in Swaziland were confined almost entirely to the *Incwala* or First Fruits ceremony. The reason for this age-old ritual is that the King and his subjects must be spiritually cleansed before they may eat of the ripening crops.

It will be recalled that by visiting the She-Elephant in 1955, the 'gates had been opened' for me. I had to wait until 1961 before going in.

I attended the *Incwala* on four occasions in the following eight years. Because the ceremony extends over a period of roughly twenty-one days, I conducted my studies in four stages, averaging five days at a time. In 1969, having arranged with Prince Makhungu to attend the climax of that year's *Incwala*, I departed for Swaziland after lunch on Christmas day.

The opening of the *Incwala* or First Fruits ceremony takes place three weeks before the summer solstice is due. Two groups of men set out bearing sacred calabashes, one heading eastwards and the other westwards. The purpose of their mission is to fetch sea and river water. This they present to the king's medicine men who mix it with portions of a slaughtered beast and selected herbs, leaves and roots to prepare a special decoction for the *Incwala*.

The ceremony itself is divided into two parts—the Little *Incwala* which begins soon after the men return with the water, and the Big *Incwala* which opens on the evening preceding the arrival of the full moon. With the launching of the Little *Incwala*, the king, accompanied by a royal medicine man and a retinue of dignitaries, enters a small enclosure called the *inhlambelo*, situated at the southern end of the Lobamba cattlefold. Next morning at daybreak he emerges, fills his mouth with the *Incwala* decoction, and spits half in the direction of the rising sun and the rest to the west. Thereafter he returns to the *inhlambelo* hut where he is to remain in seclusion.

Early on the following day Swazi men, women and children throng into the Lobamba cattlefold to sing and dance. The songs they sing are ancient hymns, the rhythm tardy, the mood sombre and the voices throaty.

Meanwhile the moon has come to life, serving as a reminder that until the day it waxes full again no one may eat of the ripening crops. Not even the king. For he is the personification of national solidarity, and must first be ritually cleansed. There are times in a man's life when he is humbled by ancient custom, and is made to realize that without an Omnipotent Presence behind the scheme of nature, there would be no source of supply. No life, no growth, no procreation.

There are many trails that lead to Lobamba—sandy roads, cattle tracks and mountain paths—and as the moon grows bigger and the Great *Incwala* draws nearer they turn into human streams adorned with feathers and fur and printed cloth. Thousands of Swazi families move with the flow, carrying *Incwala* regalia, military shields, utensils and sleeping mats; all quietly talking, humming or chanting.

And each evening as the moon rises redder, rounder and brighter, the hordes now gathered at Lobamba turn their eyes to the horizon, silently rejoicing in the thought of events to

Swazi dignitary at the annual *Incwala*
or First Fruits ceremony.

come. On the afternoon before the full moon, a large body of men, predominantly unmarried braves, set out from Lobamba for the Bulungu valley some twenty kilometres to the east. Their task is to collect branches of the *sekwane* thorntree, a species of acacia with which they will later reinforce the king's *inhlambelo* enclosure. Their departure marks the opening of the Great *Incwala*.

Reaching Lozita, one of the king's royal kraals along the way, the young men are joined by a body of warriors stationed there, and together they hurry onwards eventually reaching the valley in the light of the moon. They then set to work with choppers. There is an urgency in the way they collect the *sekwane* branches, quickly regrouping and retracing their steps at a trot to Lobamba. They dare not loiter along the way for they must reach the king by morning to present the *sekwane* for his inspection.

Should it be found that the leaves of a branch have wilted, this exposes the bearer as an adulterer and therefore unworthy of taking part in the Great *Incwala*.

Usually the branch-bearing men arrive at the outskirts of Lobamba in the light of the rising sun, and are welcomed by a surge of people: warriors loping, drums beating, bugles, kudu horns and whistles blowing; lines of men and women loudly chanting, clapping hands and caterwauling; children following in quiet procession, wide-eyed with wonder at the wild commotion. And dogs. Dogs everywhere, yapping hysterically.

Footsore and weary after the night's ordeal, the braves press into the cattlefold and await the presence of the king. Thereafter they proceed to barracks beyond the palisades to eat and rest.

On the morning of the third day squads of youths, accompanied by warriors, go out into the surrounding bush to collect branches of the *mbondvo* shrub. These they later weave into the stems of the *sekwane*, now stacked around the king's *inhlambelo*. Meanwhile an air of quiet conviviality has crept over Lobamba—people standing or sitting together in little groups outside the cattlefold, and in the royal huts and barracks warriors, dignitaries and commoners putting the final touches to their *Incwala* regalia. Some will be found combing and brushing mantles made of ox hair, others smoothing out leopard or antelope loin skins, or titivating plumed headdresses, or gently daubing their bodies with animal fat.

During the early afternoon the crowds start congregating within the cattlefolds, lining the southern section. On the opposite side, about a hundred metres away, four of the regiments muster, each magnificently dressed to conform with ancient standards, and bearing massive oxhide shields and knob-headed sticks. Slowly the warriors, singing an ancient *Incwala* hymn, start measuring a graceful dance on the cowdung floor of the cattlefold. For fully two hours they continue to sing and

Prince Siyela in *Incwala* regalia.

Entrance to the royal cattlefold
at Lobamba, where
the Bull-Killing ceremony
is held.

Members of the Swazi royal
regiments crowding
into the Lobamba cattlefold
for the Bull-Killing
ceremony.

A section of the *Incwala*
regiments dancing in
the Lobamba cattlefold.

The Lion of the Swazi, King Sobhuza II at the
First Fruits ceremony.

dance, and the king, still confined to the *inhlambelo* hut, emerges from time to time to gaze smilingly upon them. Then towards mid-afternoon a wild, black bull, escorted by a small herd of heifers, is brought into the arena by a squad of naked braves. Driven cautiously up to the gates of the *inhlambelo*, it is brought face to face with the king, who strikes it with a talismanic stick and provokes it into fury.

In 1969 I saw the bull suddenly rear, kick out wildly and then gallop away, scattering the heifers, then the braves and finally the left flank of the regiments. Pursued by the braves, it crashed into the palisades at the bottom end of the cattlefold. At that moment it was cornered and pounced upon by the squad of naked men. Bellowing frantically to the accompaniment of thudding fists on its body and the rhythmical chanting of the regiments, it was dragged slowly across the arena. At the king's enclosure, it was forced through the gateway and then stabbed to death by a medicine man. Now beyond sight of the crowds its gall bladder was removed, and hung around King Sobhuza's neck. A little later the monarch himself appeared at the gates,

swaggered across the arena, and joining the front rank of the regiments danced with his warriors until evening.

During the following three days Lobamba resounded to happy festivity. The king mingled freely with his subjects, dignitaries and commoners alike, and the She-Elephant, followed by a train of royal wives and princesses, took part from time to time in the dancing and singing. Then came the moment for the king and his queens to eat of the ripening crops, the first fruits of the season, releasing the nation from the taboo it had so far been forced to observe. A pyre was lit and on it was piled the remains of the bull, portions of the crops, as well as the king's sleeping mats, regalia and other items used by him in the *inhlambelo* enclosure.

Then the *Incwala* ceremony ended, and the trails again became human streams now flowing outwards from Lobamba to distant kraals. No longer were the first fruits forbidden. The Swazi could look forward with happy anticipation to harvest time.

In Xhosa Territory

The most southerly of the East Coast Nguni nations and, in fact, all Negro nations of Africa, are the Xhosa-speaking peoples, whose territories extend roughly from the Umtamvuna River in southern Natal to the Great Fish River in the Cape. Divided by tradition into ten large tribal units, and these in turn into a multiplicity of clans, the Xhosa were in the forefront of the Nguni nations during their migration southwards in centuries past.

Xhosa territory is largely an infinite landscape of lush, rolling pastures, much of its coastline an entanglement of sub-tropical trees, towering rocks and precipices. Studded with rondavel huts, vast patches of crimson tree-aloe and yellow-blossomed

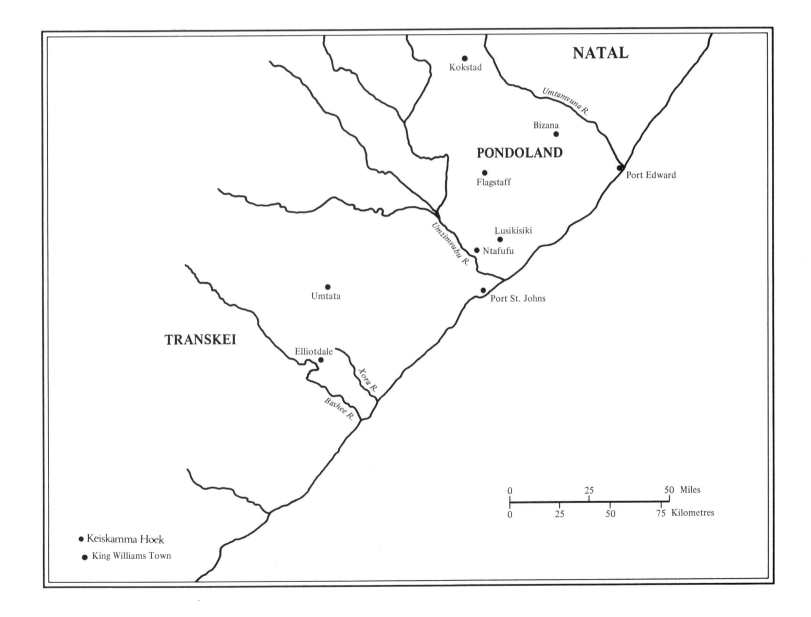

Ngqika mother and child, Ciskei.

cassia, it is criss-crossed with sheep, cattle and sled tracks and embellished in the more westerly regions with snow-capped mountain ranges.

The majority of the Xhosa have clung to a traditional mode of dress: blankets dyed red with ochre; turbans black, blue, green and purple; multi-coloured bead necklaces; copper, plastic and rubber bangles and sporran-like pouches made of jackal, genet or antelope skin. The women beautify their faces with designs in red, white and yellow clay, and like their menfolk smoke long, wooden, hand-carved pipes skilfully adorned with beads. Presumably as a result of intermarriage with Bushmen and Hottentots in distant times, the Xhosa are smaller in stature and lighter-skinned than the other East Coast tribes to the north. They are handsome people, their women considered the most beautiful of all in tribal Southern Africa.

Circumcision and Initiation

My sojourns among the Xhosa began in 1954, first in the Ciskeian territories ruled at the time by the late Paramount Chief Archie Velile Sandile, then two years later among the Pondo groups of Paramount Chiefs Victor Photo and Botha Sigcau, and finally during the 1960s in the land of the Thembu tribes of Paramount Chief Sabata Jonguhlanga Dalindyebo. The experience I gained in those parts is among the richest I have found anywhere. The opportunities given me by Xhosa dignitaries to study Xhosa customs, including the closely guarded ritual of circumcision, stand out in my mind as great privileges.

Circumcision is practised by all but a small minority of Xhosa-speaking people. Over a period of eight years I visited circumcision lodges among two of the ten Xhosa-speaking tribes—the Bomvana who inhabit the Xora and Bashee river districts, and the Ngqika in the vicinity of Keiskamma Hoek. In both areas, bearing in mind the written records of pioneer missionaries and scholars of past decades, I found only minor changes in practical procedure, and virtually no change at all in the spiritual implications of this vital aspect of Xhosa life.

Until the end of the eighteenth century circumcision formed part of the puberty rites of all major Southern African tribes. After 1816, however, the practice was abolished by King Shaka in all territories overrun by his Zulu armies. Determined to mould the motley of tribes and clans into a powerful homogeneous nation, he needed every available youth for his fighting forces. So he closed down the circumcision lodges everywhere and had the initiates brought to his military kraals for training.

At the time of his assassination in 1828, King Shaka's nets had been cast as far south as the Umzimvubu river, isolating the Pondo tribe from the rest of the Xhosa-speaking peoples. This explains why the great majority of Xhosa south of the Umzimvubu have continued to practise circumcision, and tend to this day to look askance at their uncircumcized Pondo brethren.

In other tribes of Southern Africa boys at the age of puberty are circumcized in large batches every three or four years, but in Xhosa territories lodges are opened annually, and initiates vary in age from eighteen to twenty-five. The rule is that fathers with eligible sons must apply individually to their chiefs for permission to build a lodge in a chosen area. The fathers then come together, accompanied by groups of workers, and erect a dome-shaped straw hut, the size depending on the number of youths to be housed.

The job complete, the fathers are then ordered by a fellow tribesman, recently selected as overseer to the lodge, to report with their sons on an appointed day. On arrival the youths are ushered into a sheep pen where their heads are shaved, their clothes removed and their sunken spirits uplifted by a small circle of solicitous male friends and relatives—some young, some old, but all of them circumcized in former years.

The circumcision is performed by a medicine man renowned for his dexterity with an assegai blade. Not a word is spoken, not a sound comes from the crowd as he goes about his work. And although the initiates are given no opiate to relieve their pain, they dare not betray the slightest sign of emotion. This is a vital part of the proceedings. No matter how severe the pain, they must be sure not to sigh or moan, clench a fist, twitch a toe, or even frown or blink. At all costs they must appear to be brave, for in a circumcision lodge a coward is spurned by fellow initiates, ridiculed by visitors, and consistently reprimanded by the father to whom he has caused embarrassment. Seldom, therefore, are there signs of cowardice.

From the moment of their circumcision to the day they leave the lodge, some five months later, the youths are subjected to toil and hardship. Loins aching, minds anguished and bodies stiff from tossing and turning on crude bedsteads made of branches and bamboo staves, they are roused each wintry morning at dawn. They are then driven from the hut and made to attend to their festering wounds.

They usually do this at the edge of a nearby stream where they gently wash their wounds, dress them with the soft, porous leaves of a local shrub and wrap them in the silken sheaths of a large, onion-like bulb. For about three weeks, while their wounds heal, the initiates remain confined to the lodge. They are given menial jobs by the overseer, and draped in white blankets or sheepskin karosses. Their bodies daubed with white clay as a purificatory measure, they also spend several hours basking in

Paramount Chief Sabata Dalindyebo.

The late Paramount Chief Archie Velile Sandile.

Kolisile Billi, praise-singer to Xhosa paramount chiefs.

the winter sun. Talking in whispers they dwell on the pain they have suffered together and continue to suffer; and they confide in each other about the cravings they have for a self-rolled cigarette, a pinch of snuff or a draught of beer, cravings they have to stifle. And they talk about hunger and their yearning for food, any food except the food of the lodge, which is last year's corn-on-the-cob, burnt hard like river pebbles.

Those first three weeks are so hard to bear that even the most confident and extroverted youths become suddenly withdrawn, subdued and docile. Is it not claimed by their elders that no matter how frivolous, irresponsible or delinquent a youth might be before circumcision, when once he has been broken down and taught to bow to the rigid codes of the lodge, he emerges at the end as a sober-minded, respectable adult?

The rules and restrictions of a lodge are manifold, and punishment follows swiftly on all acts of transgression, however trivial. Even the most mundane conversation can lead to trouble, for the lodge has a secret jargon of its own, which if not correctly used by initiates earns them a whipping. For example, everyday words such as hut, door, bed, mat, fire, dog, sheep pen and scores of others are replaced by exotic terms. And considering the consequences should a slip be made, it follows that mind and tongue must work together in perfect precision.

Time passes slowly in a circumcision lodge, the initiates say, but because they have been taught since childhood that pain is cured by pain itself they show no signs of impatience. During the third week their wounds become itchy and, as this is taken to mean that the thorniest part of the five-month journey has been left behind, they become a little more willing to smile. Any day now they will be sent by the overseer into the surrounding hills, valleys and woods to search for food, for tradition dictates that a man must know how to fend for himself, even if fending means stealing from outlying kraals.

So when this second stage of their ordeal arrives, the initiates leave the lodge in twos and threes, their blankets and karosses matching the white of their clay-daubed bodies. Armed with sticks, spears or battle-axes and accompanied by fleet-footed whippet-like dogs, they hunt birds and hares and even fowls that stray from the kraals. They pilfer granaries, rob fowl pens of eggs, and occasionally depending on the forgetfulness of local kraal patriarchs, help themselves to wedges of meat hung out to dry. There is only one snag about this permissible adventure into theft. Should they be caught red-handed they are thrashed, first by their captor and then later at the lodge by the overseer.

After about two months this period of roaming, hunting and stealing comes to an end, and the initiates spend most of their time back at the lodge where, among other things, they are taught the delicate steps of an ancient dance. This *kwetha* dance,

Initiates are responsible for collecting medicinal leaves, in the surroundings, for dressing their circumcision wounds.

Members of a Bomvana circumcision lodge near the Bashee River, Transkei. The flags over the hut door have been specially 'doctored' to ward off harmful influences.

Headdress worn by Ngqika initiates.

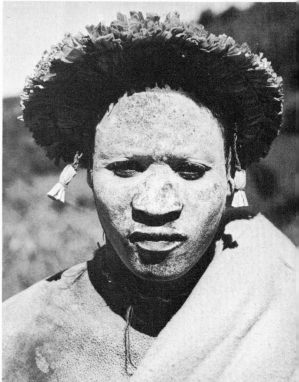

An initiate carefully selecting soft, porous leaves to be used as bandages.

Initiates' bodies are daubed with purifactory clay.

During the fortnight after
circumcision the youths
are taken on short walks
by their overseer,
in the vicinity of the lodge.

Ngqika initiates, their bodies
draped in white blankets,
found hunting in the hills
overlooking the
circumcision lodge.

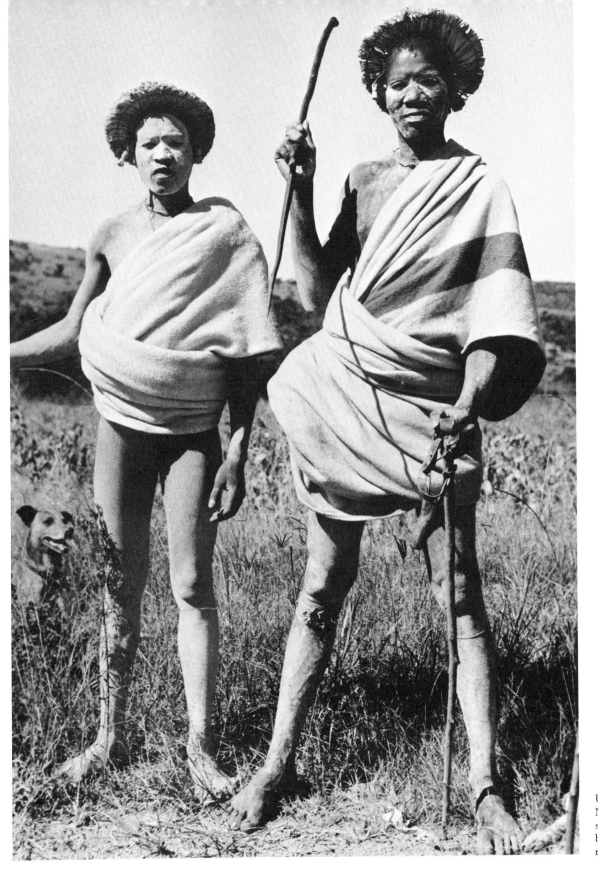

Usually initiates hunt in pairs.
Note the stabbing
spear and catapult held
by the youth on the
right.

Preparation for
the *kwetha* dance.

A Uukwambi water trough
carved from the trunk of the
ivory palm

A Ronga Kraal in the
swampy regions near
Incoluane

Regalia for the *kwetha*
dance is made of
palm leaves.

An oxhide strung across a circle of poles serves
as the drum for the *kwetha* dance.

or dance of the initiates, forms part of the ceremony at the closing
of the lodge, that longed-for day when the youths will be presented to relatives and friends as newly fledged adult men.

On the morning of their final day in the lodge the initiates
rise at cockcrow, and begin the lengthy task of decorating torso
and limb with exotic designs. With clays, mainly yellow and
red, and with soot, ash and 'washing-blue' cubes, they draw
circles, ovals, squares and triangles, all intertwined with straight,
curly or zigzag stripes. The patterns stand out vividly against
the background of bodies daubed white since the day of circumcision.

At mid-morning the initiates, assisted by attendants under
supervision of the overseer, put on their *kwetha* regalia. This
includes a mask, a lofty headdress and a voluminous ballerina-
like skirt, all made of palm fronds.

Meanwhile a noisy crowd has been gathering in the immediate
vicinity of the lodge—blanketed and turbaned relatives, friends
and acquaintances, the women and maidens bearing gifts, the

men their fighting sticks and the younger folk accompanied by
dogs. When eventually the initiates appear, lining up shoulder to
shoulder to begin the *kwetha* dance, they are greeted with cheering, whistling and the clatter of fighting sticks. Close by a group
of elderly women take up positions around an oxhide strung
across a circle of upright poles. Singing a *kwetha* song they beat
out its rhythm with sticks, pausing from time to time to take
a pinch of snuff or to enjoy a mug of sorghum beer.

The *kwetha* dance is not spectacular. No stamping of feet, no
leaping or writhing or turning about. Bodies erect and arms
held gracefully at the sides, the initiates do no more than
jerkily raise and drop their heels in time to the singing and drumming. This movement causes the heavy palm-frond skirts to
flap up and down, producing a sharp percussion sound not unlike the rattle of tambourines. And to add to the rhythm the
spectators join in, clapping their hands or smacking their fighting sticks together.

The dancing continues for at least an hour, then suddenly it

The *kwetha* dance.

is brought to a close by the overseer. The initiates now run off to the initiation lodge and quickly strip. They toss their regalia on to a pile, followed by everything else they have used during the past few months. They then go haring down to the stream close by. Plunging into the water they wash the white from their bodies, removing every trace of the clay that has clogged their skins since the day they were circumcized. Once thoroughly cleansed they daub themselves again with clay, but this time the red kind, which symbolizes their return to the tribe as men.

Meanwhile the lodge has been set alight, and although their nostrils fill with the smell of smoke and their ears with the crackle of the flames, the initiates spare their eyes the sight of the fire. This is essential if they are to avoid misfortune in the years ahead.

When the hut has burnt out, the initiates are escorted from the stream back to the place where the crowds await them. Still naked they screen themselves behind a herd of cattle. When they reach the vicinity of the smouldering hut they are given new blankets to wear, freshly dyed with red ochre.

Now they are welcomed by their relatives, sweethearts and friends, extolled as heroes and hailed as adults eligible for marriage and parenthood.

They are showered with gifts—beadwork, bangles, turbans, pipes, snuff-boxes, hunting sticks and tit-bits of food. Most of all they are showered with love. During the rest of the day they join in the feasting and dancing arranged to celebrate their return to everyday tribal life. Even the stern-faced overseer has suddenly become a smiling friend.

A succession of speeches follow, delivered by fathers and selected elders, lengthy discourses on Xhosa customs, beliefs and etiquette, on the host of responsibilities they will have to face, or on the standards of behaviour expected of them.

As I heard one old Xhosa chief put it so aptly in typical Xhosa metaphor:

'Young men, I ask you to look back on your lives. In childhood you were not unlike little worms enjoying the carefree existence

At the close of the initiation
lodge the white clay
is washed from the body
and protective amulets
worn around the neck.

of eating, eating and eating; in puberty you went into the cocoon of the circumcision lodge, and now in manhood you come out as moths ready to mate and continue the cycle of life. Spread your newly grown wings proudly but cautiously, and be mindful of the lessons you have learnt during initiation lest they be torn, clipped or even plucked.'

When a man emerges from an initiation lodge, humbled by the ordeal of circumcision and sobered by five months of enduring hardship, he no longer has thought for trivial matters.

So the Xhosa say.

Khotso, Millionaire Psychic

On 25 July 1972 three arresting words were flashed over South African radio, featured prominently as newspaper headlines, and in the weeks to follow bandied by Africans from Cape Town to Messina on the Limpopo river. Just three words: 'Khotso is dead!'

I met Khotso in the winter of 1958. I had been researching at that time among the Abelungu clan of the Pondoland Wild Coast, and travelling one evening along a dirt road on my way to Port St Johns my truck broke down on the outskirts of a place marked on the map as Ntafufu. Delighted to be so close to what I imagined was a little village, I was soon to find that Ntafufu consisted of no more than a solitary trading store.

I had just lifted the bonnet of the truck when suddenly my attention was drawn to an approaching convoy of motor cars headed by a chauffeur-driven Cadillac. Moments later the cars skidded to a halt abreast of me throwing up clouds of dust, and from out of them stepped about twenty African men headed by the owner of the Cadillac. He was a short, thickset man dressed in robes that reached down to his feet.

'You have trouble?' he asked, addressing me in Xhosa.

'Yes,' I replied, and before I could muster another word he called over his shoulder to one of his men.

'Xaba!' he bellowed, 'hey, Xaba! Come, man, come, have a look at this engine!'

'My name is Khotso,' he continued, turning to me, then pointing to a young man clad in grease-stained overalls added with a grin: 'Xaba has a love for machinery like the rest of these fellows have a love for food.'

'Khotso!' I cried, 'you're Khotso Sethuntsa?'

'That's right,' he smiled, 'so you've heard of me?'

Of course I had heard of Khotso Sethuntsa, Khotso the millionaire psychic, the most publicized herbalist, diviner and exorcizer in Southern Africa. So I told him briefly about the trips I had made into African territories, and the better-known African personages I had met.

'Then you were meant to be stuck in Ntafufu,' he said, chuckling now, 'which also means you must come to my place tomorrow.'

I hesitated, recalling arrangements I had made to visit a retired missionary in Port St Johns in the morning.

'There can be no refusing,' he cried, 'because otherwise I will order Xaba to make a mess of that engine, and you'll have to continue the journey through the mountains by donkey cart.'

But I had no real intention of refusing. For far too long I had wanted to meet this colourful man. I assured him I would be happy to come and that I believed our meeting had been pre-ordained.

Within ten minutes my truck was again in running order. No sooner had Xaba slammed down the bonnet and wiped his hands than Khotso gave orders for his retinue to return to the cars and follow him home. The convoy moved slowly down the road, veered off to the right through the bush and disappeared from sight.

I slept that night at the trading store at the insistence of the owner, who had come down to greet me a moment after Khotso's departure. Next morning I took leave of my host at about nine o'clock, and soon my thoughts were dancing to the purr of the truck as it bounced and skipped along a narrow track leading to Khotso's place. Ten minutes later I entered a short avenue of banana palms, at the top end of which was a wooden swing-gate guarded on either side by a bevy of watchmen. After a momentary stop to greet them I crept slowly onwards between rows of men dressed in blankets. Then suddenly I caught sight of an old-fashioned red-roofed house. This was Khotso's house.

My arrival was announced by a party of Khotso's attendants, some cheering, others beating drums or blowing whistles. No sooner had I emerged from the truck than I was met by an elderly dignitary and led along a pathway flanked with white-painted stones to Khotso's house. A cluster of women all clad in flowing white robes came forward to greet me, singing and clapping their hands in lively rhythm.

Then Khotso appeared at the doorway. He wore a silver robe, beautifully patterned with embroidered flowers and sprinkled with sequins which glittered in the morning sun. A long-legged dog, its coat matted and moth-eaten in parts, stood at his side, blissfully threshing its tail. As I reached the step where Khotso waited I paused, sensing he had something to say before inviting me in. Suddenly to my surprise he turned around, and raising a hand to his mouth cried out:

'Langa! Langa! We are waiting for you!'

Khotso, millionaire psychic.

Khotso, his son Langa
and attendants in 1958.

Langa, I was to learn a few seconds later, was a little light-skinned boy, one of Khotso's numerous sons. Stepping coyly forward from behind his father, he stood looking at me with doleful eyes.

'Go and greet our visitor,' Khotso said, and the boy curtsying shyly and taking hold of my hands gently pressed a kiss on each. Next moment Khotso himself was standing beside me, and together we entered his home, stepping into a small, shadowy living room, the walls panelled with mirrors and the floor spread over with lion, eland and zebra skins. Showing me to a chair he clapped his hands sharply together, and in a loud voice ordered a servant to bring tea and biscuits. He then settled on a bench beside me, and for a short while our conversation turned to the circumstances that had brought us together the day before.

When the refreshments arrived we moved to a table in the centre of the room, where I set out a selection of photographs of tribal peoples I had brought to show him. As his eyes moved from one picture to another his face lit up with delight. He showed particular interest in a portrait I had taken of a headman named Speelman, whose village was situated in the bushy regions thirty kilometres north of Pretoria.

'Did you say his name was Speelman?' he asked.

I nodded.

'Then this means he is a relative of mine, because he bears my father's name, and my father himself was born in those parts.'

'Khotso,' I ventured, 'I have a favour to ask of you. I would like to know more about your father and your earlier life. Very little has been written about how you became Southern Africa's best-known psychic.'

'I will tell you all,' he replied, 'so that you can write my story one day.'

I switched on a tape recorder I had brought for this very purpose.

'I have a deep love for Pretoria,' Khotso began, 'a love as deep as a bottomless well. My father, Speelman, loved it too, but his well was even deeper than mine. You see, his mind was rich with the life he had spent there; my mind had to gather its riches from the stories I heard from my mother.

'Long before I was born my father worked for President Paul Kruger, first as a stable-boy, then as a coachman, and then in later life both as a coachman and as a personal servant. Now, at that time, there was a chief called Mapasa who lived with his followers in the Herschel district, on the border of the Orange Free State. Mapasa was a clever man, very clever, for how else could he have become the biggest stock thief in those parts and survived the Boer farmers' guns? He was also säid to be wise, which I believe he wasn't, because a man of wisdom knows better than to lead a life of theft and killing.

'Anyhow, one day, not many years before the war between Paul Kruger's Boers and the British, the old president paid a visit to the president of the Free State, Hendrik Brand, taking my father with him. Among the many things they talked about was the problem of Mapasa's stealing. It therefore came about that they decided to send my father, Speelman, to visit the chief and get him to end his thieving ways.

'So Speelman eventually arrived on the outskirts of Herschel where he was quickly captured by Mapasa's men and condemned to death as a spy. But like myself, my father was gifted with a way of speaking that caused men to listen and understand. Soon therefore he became the chief's own guest, and not very long after that, his son-in-law. Because, although by now my father was free, his heart had been imprisoned by Mokholistoana, Mapasa's daughter. They married, and when the time came for Speelman to leave he took Mokholistoana with him to Pretoria. There they were welcomed by President Kruger, who had long given up hope that my father would ever return.

'In 1897 Paul Kruger received a message from Brand that the problems with Mapasa had ceased. And because it so happened that I was born at that time, the old president insisted that my father call me Vrede, which in English is Peace and in our language Khotso. So that's how I got my name.

'Shortly after my birth my mother started working for Mrs Kruger, carrying me always on her back. She was happy as a servant except that her name had to be changed to Khaki, after the khaki clothing she was given to wear. This was simply because Mrs Kruger's tongue went lame whenever it had to say "Mokholitsoana".

'Then came the war between the Boers and the English, and fearing we would come to harm we were sent by Speelman, my mother and I, back to the kraal of Chief Mapasa. That was the end of Pretoria. We never returned, and never set eyes on my father again. Some said he was killed in the war, and others that he was appointed headman over a clan near Pretoria when the fighting stopped. Which is why I believe the headman called Speelman now living in those parts must be related to us.'

While Khotso spoke I had been making notes in a pocket book about items of interest around us. I had noted, for example, a bust of Paul Kruger crudely fashioned in river clay, and painted with household enamel. Placed conspicuously on a wicker stand it was flanked by well-known, historical photographs of President Kruger, all of them framed in gilted wood.

'Can you remember Kruger,' I asked, 'considering how young you were when the war broke out?'

'Remember?' he bellowed, 'I don't have to remember because I see him almost every day.'

'I don't understand,' I said, although suspecting he was alluding to his gift of clairvoyance.

'I'll tell you,' he replied, 'but to tell you properly I must go back to my childhood days. You see, when I was a child at Mapasa's kraal, the old president used to appear to me in my dreams. Then one night he came when my eyes were open, and my body went cold and shook with fear.

'I spoke to my mother and Mapasa about it, and both of them said they were glad. Because now they knew I had been blessed with the gift for "seeing", and that Paul Kruger was still our friend. I then started seeing him about once a month, then once a week and then once a day or more. And eventually Mapasa died, and later my mother, and they both warned me as they were dying to keep close to the spirit of President Kruger. This I have done, so you see I haven't had to think of my childhood days in Pretoria to remember him.

'I became a hunter at the age of fifteen, and one day in the hills whilst stalking a jackal he, the old president, appeared suddenly to me. "Khotso," he said, "when you grow up you'll be very rich, but your greatest riches will come from your mind." I was puzzled! What could this mean? What was I to do? I just went on hunting year after year, hunting and skinning, until one day the skins I had saved were enough for two wagons to carry. Hundreds of them—jackal, antelope and even leopard. I sold them one day to a trader in Kokstad, and with the money I started building the first part of the house that later became my mansion there.

'Meanwhile I had learnt the art of herbalism, and had also discovered I had been blessed with the gift of healing the sick, not only with my medicines but also with the spirit of life that works through healing hands. Now I felt within me a peacefulness, knowing that our Great Creator had many things for me to do. "This is the riches of the mind," I was told one night in a dream, "the kind that makes the poorest man feel wealthy, and the wealthy wealthier still."

'As news of my healing gifts began to spread, so too did the herbs I sold turn into money. My home in Kokstad grew bigger and bigger, and I found myself surrounded by many followers. In a way this troubled me, because I was an ordinary person of ordinary parents, and I believed only chiefs were entitled to followers.

'It was a cold winter's evening in Kokstad, when the mountains around were deep in snow, when I was visited by an old man from Matatiele. He was sick and wet and frozen, and he asked to be healed. He slept at my home that night, and with the help of He-Who-Knows-All he was made to feel better. Next morning the old man said to me: "Khotso, your gift of healing belongs not only to you, not only to us in these parts, but to all mankind. So, my son, soon you will have to start going from place to place, and especially to distant parts where men and women cry out for healing." I was amazed by these words, because not two days before a voice within me had said: "Khotso, remember a caterpillar never remains with one leaf alone, or one twig, or even one branch. Take heed of its habits and for sure your riches will multiply."

'So with the money I was making from herbalism I bought cattle, selling them for profit, and then buying and selling all over again until I could see I was becoming rich. Soon I was able to buy a farm, and then another and another, until today, as we sit here talking together, I have twelve farms which keep bringing me riches I never thought I would have.

'And each year, as the trees grow bigger and their leaves more plentiful, I know, like the caterpillar, I have to go farther and farther, travelling to share my gifts with all who need them. And just as important has been the need to teach others to heal, which is the reason why right here in Ntafufu I have dozens of students from all over Southern Africa, and from countries far beyond the Zambezi River.

'This is my story. This is the life I will follow until the day I am called to the life yet to come.'

In the years since my first visit to Ntafufu, much has been written and spoken about Khotso, with particular reference to his inestimable wealth. The publicity has not always been complimentary, for although dozens of journalists could claim to have met him, only a handful could really claim to have fathomed his character. His critics, therefore, should not be blamed for exposing his flair for showmanship, nor should they be criticized for drawing attention to the boyish pleasure he derived from conducting tourists through the somewhat grotesquely designed, oriental-style home he built at Lusikisiki. It is true that he was heard to speak boastfully about the multiplicity of his assets—the fifty-one farms he was reputed eventually to own, the tremendous profits he had derived from innumerable property deals, the limousines and buses he had bought for carrying his wives, children and followers when he travelled from place to place, and the lucrative trade he conducted in cattle and horses. It is also true that he made no effort to deny that a dungeon he had had built in his house was stacked not only with cannisters and trunks containing what he called 'available cash', but also with packets of cut diamonds acquired in the course of the years. Indeed, he had even allowed journalists to announce his intention of buying the entire town of Lusikisiki, well knowing it was not for sale.

Beneath this veneer of boastfulness was another Khotso, gentle and kind, considerate and generous. It was an alter-ego

Khotso's attendants grinding medicines whilst
patients in the background await attention.

that generated a current of powerful love, that served not only to enliven his own personality but to bring joy to the lives of all who needed his help. In the words of Paramount Chief Velile Sandile, who knew him well: 'In the same way that he keeps his scalp clean-shaven and shiny, so too does he keep his mind clear and bright, and shaven of harmful thought.'

To return to Khotso's living room at Ntafufu. Having told me his story he rose from the table, moved to the open door and, adjusting his regalia like an opera star poised to come on stage from the wings, he stepped into the sunlight. His sudden appearance was greeted with an outburst of exultation from scores of devotees who had meanwhile gathered outside his home. They hailed him for at least a minute, and as he swaggered slowly down the pathway towards them they broke into happy song. I followed close on his heels to the side of the house and along a pergola leading to a wooden doorway. By this time the singing had ceased and there was silence once more.

Reaching the door Khotso paused, bowed his head in prayer, then moved on and entered a courtyard encircled by a hedge of poinsettia and bougainvillea. To the right of us was a row of kneeling women, all of them identically dressed in white, and employed in grinding medicinal herbs, roots and barks with grinding stones. To the left, seated on benches, were about thirty patients awaiting Khotso's arrival. During the following two hours I watched as one by one they came forward to confer with him. Some had bodily ailments while others were troubled by anxieties stemming from psychic experiences they had had. They all asked for medicine, which he gave them in return for a small fee. One old man had brought two teenage sons whom he declared were habitually delinquent and in need of medicine to restore them to normal, responsible youths. It was in his dealings with this man that I was to witness an aspect of Khotso's nature unfamiliar to me, part of the inner self which he was inclined to conceal beneath those flamboyant robes.

'So you say your boys are rogues,' he said to the father.

'Yes,' the old man replied.

'But why?'

'I cannot say.'

'But surely you should know, if only because it is not uncommon for the markings on calves to resemble the markings of the bull that sired them.'

'This I do know.'

'Then do you agree that it is sometimes the father who must be blamed for the waywardness of his sons?'

'Yes, I agree that it can be so.'

'Then remembering how long I have known you, my friend, my advice is that you should first look into your own heart, and consider the path you wanted your sons to walk, but neglected yourself to walk.

'Is it not true that you have been unduly hard on your sons?' Khotso continued, placing a friendly hand on the old man's shoulder.

'Perhaps it is true,' the old man nodded.

'So it is well to remember that if a herdsman unduly kicks his calves, they grow up to kick him back.'

Turning to the boys Khotso enquired if they had ever eaten their own vomit.

'No,' they cried, taken aback.

'Then why do you behave like mongrels? Is it just because you are a little wiser than mongrels are? No, my sons, it is not mongrels you must aim to be, but bulls of the herd. But when young bulls are unruly we shorten their horns, just as yours will be shortened if you don't begin to mend your ways.'

Drawing the old father aside Khotso assured him that delinquency could not be cured with medicines. What the two boys needed most was love and encouragement. In the same way that all birds must come to roost after flying, he concluded, so even the most restless youths settle down in adulthood.

His consultations over for the morning, Khotso led me to a section of the courtyard obscured by a tall reed hedge. There I found three groups of men sorting out piles of medicinal roots, herbs and bark, which they packed into cardboard boxes. These men, he explained, were students who had come to him not only from various parts of Southern Africa, but also from countries as remote as Malawi. When they were not sorting medicines, he continued, they made goatskin neck, wrist and ankle amulets for prospective clients. Having enjoyed his tutelage for just over a year, the students also spent much of their time dispensing a great variety of medicines, the most popular of which was a yellow, sweet-smelling aphrodisiac called *ibangalala*.

'This is a great seller all over the country,' he said, 'so great that we often run short of supplies.'

'Is it in such great demand?' I asked.

'For sure it is, you must remind me to give you some,' he replied.

'And do you take *ibangalala*?' I teased.

'Every day,' he said, becoming suddenly serious. 'That's why my body is young, and my mind gives no thought to my age in years.'

From the courtyard we returned to the house through a side door, and entering the kitchen, then the dining room and later one of his many bedrooms he introduced me to eight of his wives. They were dressed alike in long, yellow gowns in the fashion of the Kruger era—high-waisted, tight-sleeved and with necklines that reached to the Adam's apple. Shy and seemingly

Khotso, the famous psychic, acknowledging
the acclamation of his students.

awe-struck by our sudden appearance, they curtsied politely, making a jingling sound with the strings of bells that Khotso insisted they wore around their necks. It was well past midday by now, so Khotso and I sat down to a meal of roast chicken, cabbage and gravy.

In the afternoon, after Khotso had taken his customary nap, I told him about the missionary I had arranged to meet in Port St Johns, and that I would have to leave well before sunset to ensure crossing the mountains before nightfall. He became instantly offended. Had I not enjoyed his company, he barked, and had I not found his place worthy of my presence? He had hoped I would stay until the following day at least, but, on second thoughts, would agree to my going provided I called in at Ntafufu on my way back to Johannesburg.

This I promised to do, and we parted with a pledge that hence-forth we would remember each other as kindred spirits. A week later I returned to Ntafufu, but Khotso had left for his 'mansion', as he called his rambling home in Kokstad.

Before his death in the winter of 1972, I was to revisit Khotso Sethuntsa six times, at Ntafufu, Kokstad or Lusikisiki. In all that time, despite his riches and mounting fame, I could detect no change in his disposition worthy of note. At our second meeting (this took place in 1959, at Ntafufu) I had the unexpected privilege of being inducted into what he called his *Izindaba Zethu*, or inner circle. It was a lengthy ceremony, starting in the early afternoon and ending at sunset. I emerged elated from it all, confessing to him how proud I felt, which was perhaps why he made me swear on oath never to divulge a single detail of what had occurred.

The regalia he gave me to wear on that memorable occasion hangs today in the research museum at my home, KwaVulindlela. It serves to remind me not so much of Khotso, Southern Africa's most publicized herbalist, diviner and exorcizer, as of the Khotso who was happiest when he could withdraw from the luxury of his Kokstad or Lusikisiki 'mansions' to some far-off retreat like Ntafufu; not so much of Khotso the millionaire psychic, whose business acumen had led to a daily distribution of his remedies by some two hundred travelling salesmen, as of the far less-known Khotso who gave donations to charity and secret aid to the poor; not so much of the patriarch who could boast of a harem of twenty-four wives and over two hundred children, as of the man whose facility for brotherly love extended far beyond his family circle to virtually all who came into his life; not so much of the mystical figure whose funeral attracted thousands of mourners of every race, his coffin identical to the one in which the late President John Kennedy was laid to rest, as of the devotee who spoke earnestly of death as merely the transition of the soul to a higher life.

No, the regalia he gave me brings to mind the Khotso I learned to know backstage, as it were, where he was free to pursue the spiritual life he cherished, far out of reach of sightseers who tended to gape at him as if he were a circus freak.

Not least of all, it reminds me of a short, thickset man, his head shaven and his body draped in robes, who came to my assistance along a dirt road on the way to Port St Johns.

KwaZulu

King Cyprian: His Life, Death and Burial

Between the Transkeian territories and Swaziland and to the immediate north of Natal lies the land of the Zulu nation. It is a country rich in the violent grandeur of forest, bushveld and mountain range, and rich in the tranquillity that pervades its valleys, gorges, rivers and plains. Its beauty is reflected in the very name it bears—KwaZulu, Place of Heaven.

During the first decade of the nineteenth century, KwaZulu was inhabited by scores of clans all pursuing a similar culture, all speaking a similar language, but all distinctively named and ruled by independent hereditary chieftains. Among the smallest of the clans was the Zulu or People of Heaven, whose territory spanned the White Umfolozi and Umhlatuze rivers, and whose ruler, Senzangakhona, was to sire a number of famous sons, among them the redoubtable Shaka.

In 1816 Chief Senzangakhona died, and although the succession now fell to his heir, Sigujana, the throne was usurped by Shaka, who had meanwhile risen to prominence as a warrior and political leader of uncommon ability. No sooner had the dust he stirred up settled than Shaka mustered a small fighting force and embarked on the subjugation of the neighbouring clans. During the following twelve years he extended his rule over a vast territory bordered by the Pongolo River in the north and Pondoland's farthest boundary, the Umzimvubu river, in the south. A man not only of might but also of extraordinary foresight, he was to become revered as the founder and architect of the powerful Zulu nation, and the first of its several illustrious kings.

King Shaka, it will be recalled, was murdered by his half-brother, Dingane, who succeeded him as King of the Zulu in 1828. Dingane in turn succumbed to an assassin's blade following a turbulent reign of twenty-two years. The Izingonyama or Lions who ruled after him were installed in the following years: Mpande KaSenzangakhona—1840; Cetshawyo KaMpande—1872; Dinuzulu KaCetshwayo—1898; Solomon Nkayishana Maphumzana—1916 and Nyangayezizwe Cyprian Bhekuzulu—1948. It was the last of these Lions, the ailing King Cyprian, whose life the She-Elephant of Swaziland had predicted would become part of my own. Indeed for over a decade I was to share with others close to him the sadness that plagued his declining years.

King Cyprian was born and weaned in the Nsindeni royal kraal in the KwaZulu district of Mahlabathini. His mother, Queen Ntombeni, was the first and most senior of forty royal women taken in marriage by the previous ruler, King Solomon. She was a woman of notable character, regal almost to a fault, and despite a quiet disposition was very popular in royal circles.

KwaZulu, a country of rolling hills and scattered kraals.

148

A Zulu herdboy watches
the cows being driven
into the cattlefold
for milking.

A Bomvana initiate dressing
his wounds with medicinal
leaves

Dancing girls at King
Zwelithini's coronation

Zulu cattle, a hardy breed.

A Zulu married woman.
The hill in the background
is Isandlwana, where
Lord Chelmsford's
British army was
annihilated by the
Zulu in January, 1879.

Opposite page
Zulu matrons wear
oxhide aprons, heavily
daubed with fat.
Headdresses vary
from clan to clan.

Senior wife of a Zulu
patriarch in the
Babanango district.

Zulu grandmother on the site of King Shaka's
original Gibixhegu military kraal.

Below Grave of Nandi, King Shaka's mother.

A Zulu kraal in the Mahlabathini district.

Much of her tender nature was later to be reflected in the heir she had borne the nation.

During his infancy Cyprian moved with his mother from Nsindeni to the great Osuthu royal kraal in the Nongoma district. On entering childhood he was taken to Mahashini, Place of Horses, where he lived in his father's capital royal kraal, Dlamahlahla. At the age of seven he was enrolled as a pupil at the Mpumalanga school, remaining there until he had passed the sixth standard. As time would reveal, those early years, and in particular the years that conveyed him through adolescence into manhood, were to be the happiest of his otherwise tragic life. Carefree years spent with a group of royal companions of his own age, among whom were his half-brother, Prince Matthews Zulu, later to become widely known as the king's 'funny man', and also his cousin and closest friend, Chief Gatsha Buthelezi.

Although shy and reserved and given to spells of moodiness, the young Prince Cyprian was a manly lad who entered readily into the various activities enjoyed by his royal companions. He was a gifted soccer player whose knack for 'slicing the opposition into little pieces', in the words of Chief Buthelezi, earned him the nickname of *Busha,* the Butcher. He was also named the 'Royal Barber' by the inhabitants of Dlamahlahla, whose hair he both cut and styled when hair clippers were first introduced to KwaZulu. Perhaps the most endearing feature of his somewhat subdued personality was the way he laughed 'from the hollows of the heart' (in the Zulu phrase). And he could laugh just as easily at himself as at the witticisms of Prince Matthews Zulu or the jests of the young Buthelezi.

At the death of King Solomon in 1933, Prince Cyprian was nine years old, so a regent named Prince Mshiyeni KaDinuzulu was placed on the Zulu throne. In accordance with Zulu tradition Mshiyeni became the young prince's guardian, keeping a constant watch over the royal cub earmarked as the future Ingonyama, or Lion, of the nation. Small wonder therefore that under his critical surveillance Prince Cyprian soon became steeped in royal etiquette and protocol. Indeed, so rigid were the standards of behaviour set and demanded by the regent at Dlamahlahla that the prince and his royal companions quaked at the thought of offending him. As a child he was often punished by the stern regent, and even on reaching the verge of manhood was *sjambokked* (whipped with a heavy whip made of rhinoceros or hippopotamus hide) one day for daring to flirt with a teenage girl of the local school. Life at Dlamahlahla was seldom easy, but is had one redeeming feature—it welded the young inmates into a bond of friendship which has remained intact to this day.

During his early twenties Prince Cyprian married Princess Priscilla Masuku, and then soon afterwards Princess Thomo of the Nongoma district. At about that time the question of suc-

cession to the Zulu throne, left vacant in 1933 by the death of King Solomon Maphumzana, started to engage the minds of the Zulu royal house. Although Cyprian was recognized by most of the royal men as their future monarch, the young man's right to the kingship was contested by a small but influential faction who favoured his half-brother, Prince Absalom Thandayiphi, another of the late King Solomon's sons. In recent times Prince Cyprian had stirred up a storm of controversy at Dlamahlahla. He had fallen in love with his former teacher, a divorcée whom most of the royal family fervently disliked. Firmly entangled in the web she was said to have spun for him, he was subjected to constant rebuke by a formidable body of elders. This caused him deep concern, but not as much as the news that a lesser lion, his brother Prince Absalom, had been seen to prowl round the Zulu throne. It is said that Cyprian moped, and eventually withdrew into the dark of despair.

In the following months, as the royal elders, the councillors of the nation, argued and squabbled and debated his future, Prince Cyprian sought relief for his inner sufferings in alcohol. Until that time it had not been his custom to drink more frequently, or more assiduously, than his personal circle of drinking friends. Alcohol had not yet sunk its claws into his sensitive soul. What added to his unhappiness was the air of secrecy that enveloped the meetings of elders regularly convened by the regent, Mshiyeni. There were times when his patience was stretched almost to the point of snapping, and when he openly succumbed to tears. Since reaching manhood he had had no more ardent wish than to be crowned Lion of the Zulu.

Meanwhile his mother, Queen Ntombeni, had unearthed a letter purported to have been written by the late King Solomon, and naming Prince Cyprian as the rightful heir to the throne. But far from serving to end the dispute, it led to even more heated dissension and eventually to deadlock. In due course the nation itself started taking sides, and rumours of impending bloodshed swept KwaZulu.

It was then that the regent appealed to the South African government to arbitrate. Soon afterwards, therefore, Major Piet van der Byl, then the minister of native affairs, arrived in KwaZulu, and after lengthy deliberation with heads of the rival factions decided in favour of Prince Cyprian. And so in 1948 the 'Royal Barber' was installed at Dlamahlahla as Lion of the Zulu nation. Peace returned quickly to KwaZulu, but it was to return only in part to the life of the newly crowned king.

During the first year of his rule, King Cyprian's domestic problems multiplied. As a result of a continued association with his lover, the teacher, he had become estranged from his queens, Priscilla Masuku and Thomo. In July 1948 Queen Thomo had

A Zulu kraal, Nkwalini district.

Zulu drummer takes a short rest between dances performed by a troupe of men and women.

160 Trails and Tribes in Southern Africa

borne him a son (Queen Priscilla had had only daughters) and the king had named him Zwelithini, What Does the World Have to Say? In this way he reminded his former enemies of the victory he had won over Prince Absalom, and the acclaim he had received in most parts of KwaZulu.

The Lion had not been long on the throne when both his queens died. Marrying his teacher friend, despite the persistent disapproval of the royal house, he left Dlamahlahla. He now moved into a royal kraal recently built for him near the hamlet of Nongoma, naming it Khethomthandayo, Choose Whom You Like.

Chief Gatsha Buthelezi

My first visit to Khethomthandayo was in July 1954. It was neat, but small and unimpressive—five rondavel-shaped huts built side by side, a modest bungalow occupied by the king and his family, a palisade cattlefold and an outhouse roofed with corrugated iron. Nothing else.

The late King Cyprian, Lion of the Zulu nation.

Meeting the king in the living room of his home, I could sense an aura of dejection about him. He was nevertheless a fine-looking man. Lighter in complexion than the average Zulu, his cheeks adorned with mustachios, he was tall and erect and dressed in a brown double-breasted suit. He had a stately bearing, as one would expect of Zulu royalty, and in contrast to the broken-down man he was to become in the years ahead he looked the essence of physical health. I remained with him for only an hour, receiving his permission to research among the Zulu in the Nongoma district.

During the next two years I returned to Khethomthandayo on four occasions. Then in February 1957 I came again and presented the king with a copy of my book *Sandy Tracks* in which I had briefly written about him and, of course, the Zulu people. I paid him a further visit in September of the same year, only to find him indisposed and unable to see me. He nevertheless sent a councillor with a message that he wanted me to call on his cousin in the Mahlabathini district, his life-long friend Chief Gatsha Buthelezi. So I headed for KwaPhindangene, The Place One Returns To, Buthelezi's royal residence. I had had no opportunity of arranging an interview with the chief, and wondered if I would be welcome, considering we had not met before.

On arrival at the gates of KwaPhindangene I was led by a councillor to Chief Gatsha's European-style home. I had barely knocked on the door than it opened, and the chief stepped out on to the verandah, a book in his right hand and a smile so engaging that I knew in an instant I would indeed be welcome at The Place One Returns To. Introducing myself, I noticed Buthelezi was taken aback.

'Good Lord!' he exclaimed, 'this is a wonderful omen; I have been reading your book, *Sandy Tracks*, since early this morning, and was in fact on page ninety-six when I heard your knock.'

And a wonderful omen it has proved to be. For since that day to this our friendship, like a great *marulla*, has borne an abundance of fruit which we have constantly shared and relished.

After that first meeting I was often to visit Buthelezi at Kwa-Phindangene, and especially during the years I was writing *Path of Blood* and *Rule of Fear*. For the chief's mother, Princess Magogo uZulu, daughter of the late King Dinuzulu, was the acknowledged doyen of Zulu chroniclers, and she had promised to help me sift fact from fiction in some of the material I had gathered. So the *marulla* grew steadily loftier, and its fruit more plentiful.

Meanwhile disturbing news had been filtering into KwaZulu from out of Khethomthandayo—King Cyprian was said to have

Chief Gatsha Buthelezi.

Zulu warriors and maidens gather to take part
in a dance at KwaPhindangene, Chief Gatsha
Buthelezi's royal residence.

Waiting for the signal, KwaPhindangene royal
residence.

The dance begins.

Veteran warrior and councillor, Mthunzini
Buthelezi.

become chronically ill, and his marriage to be heading for ruin.
In addition there were whispers, furtive and ominous, that his
soul was being clawed apart in a desperate struggle with alcohol.

It was not long before the proverbial tongues began wagging
even beyond the borders of KwaZulu. Rumours spread that the
king had been seen tipsy at public gatherings, some of them
founded on fact, but by far the majority mischievously conceived
in the minds of irresponsible outsiders. Gradually King Cyprian
became an object of disparagement, and Zulu royalty seethed
with indignation. In a letter to me, Buthelezi expressed both
anger at the pitilessness of the gossip-mongers and concern
for the king's reputation. He confessed that since awakening to

the fact that the Lion, his oldest friend, seemed to be sinking into
the quicksands of doom, his heart had never ceased to ache.

I visited KwaZulu at the beginning of March 1964, and on
arrival at Khethomthandayo was told that the king had recently
been taken seriously ill. He had been rushed to the Benedictine
Missionary Hospital in the valley below Nongoma. There was
also talk that he had been bewitched and some people feared he
might even die.

From Nongoma I headed for KwaPhindangene and spent a
short while with Buthelezi. With his blessing I began to research
in the kraal of an elderly patriarch called Mthunzini, the Shadow,
a veteran councillor of the Buthelezi clan. Two days later I

received a message from Chief Gatsha to call in at Kwa Phindangene at my first opportunity. He had a matter of extreme urgency to discuss with me.

On the evening of the same day I reached his home. He looked troubled, his voice soft and shaky. King Cyprian's illness, he told me, had given rise to intrigue in some parts of KwaZulu and he, Buthelezi, had been summoned to a meeting of the royal council on the previous day. Among the decisions taken was one that I be asked to appoint a medical specialist of my own choice to examine the Lion.

Assuring Buthelezi I would be delighted to help, I promised that on my return to Johannesburg I would confer with Mr Pieter Theron, one of Southern Africa's most eminent surgeons. Theron was an authority on liver cirrhosis, I added, the very condition all of us knew the king had contracted some years before, but which we had discreetly avoided discussing.

On my return home a week later I discussed the king's dilemma with Theron, and arranged a tentative appointment for 30 March. Informing Buthelezi by telegram, he replied that the Lion, although recently discharged from hospital, would be unable to leave KwaZulu for at least a month, because of previous commitments. Then a little later a letter arrived from the chief:

'I was with my cousin yesterday,' he wrote, 'and he has not yet fixed a date…I will let you know as soon as he gives it to me.' In April he wrote again, letting us know that the king would not be available until the end of May. Finally I received the following note from him, dated 5 May: 'I have since writing to you received a phone call from him [the king]…stating that he will be in Johannesburg on 4 June for certain.' I conveyed the message to Pieter Theron.

I met King Cyprian, his secretary Walter Kanye, Chief Buthelezi and a small retinue of other dignitaries in Johannesburg on the morning of the appointed day, and together we proceeded to Theron's consulting rooms, at the Medical Centre in Jeppe Street. Little could we guess at the time that this was to be the happiest day the Lion had had in many a year.

King Cyprian and Buthelezi felt in harmony with Theron from the moment they met him. What impressed them most, I was later to learn, was his elegant yet humble manner. He was the kind of person the Zulu royal family had always been proud to count among its imposing list of friends.

The examination took place in full view of the dignitaries, in accordance with royal protocol. It was a lengthy, painstaking procedure, followed by X-ray and blood tests, and, when finally the results came to hand, by five anxious minutes while we waited for Theron to announce his findings.

The king, Theron told us, was in better condition than had been generally thought. True, the sugar content of his blood was abnormally high, but this he felt could be controlled under supervision of the doctors at the mission hospital. Coming to the liver, he explained that although swollen it was not excessively damaged, presumably because in recent months it had been spared the rigours of alcohol. Apparently King Cyprian had had pains in the abdominal region. These were not caused so much by a faulty liver as by a 'fairly large diaphragmatic hernia of a sliding type'. In future, therefore, he would be advised to sleep 'in a semi-sitting position in order to avoid reflex of acid during the night'. He, Theron, believed there was no immediate need for surgery. He would prefer 'to try conservative treatment' for a period of three months, after which, on further examination, a decision could be taken as to what action was necessary. In short, provided the king continued to abstain from alcohol, or, if need be, strictly confined his drinking to moderate quantities of the traditional sorghum beer, he could retrieve much of the health and happiness he had lost, and look forward to a long reign as monarch of the Zulu nation.

Theron's conclusions were received with jubilation.

'God has been kind to us this day,' said Chief Buthelezi, and the rest of the party replied with the royal salute—'*Bayete*!'

Now for a short while we conversed happily about many things, none of them really important but reflecting a profound spirit of thankfulness. We puffed at cigarettes together, even those of us who did not smoke. And we joked and laughed together as if the king had never been ill. Then came the time to leave, and we rose from our seats. To our astonishment, on reaching the door one of the dignitaries asked Theron for an aphrodisiac.

'Aphrodisiac did you say?' cried the surgeon, a mischievous glint in his eyes, 'No,' he said, 'this is one kind of medicine I wish I had, for believe me it is something I urgently need for myself.'

We roared with laughter, the king loudest of all.

'By the way,' added the surgeon, 'could I ask you to do me a special favour?'

'For sure,' the dignitary replied.

'If in your search,' said Theron, 'you chance to come across a good aphrodisiac, a really powerful one, please keep a little for me.'

The laughter was even louder now, and we left in this happy mood.

On the following morning King Cyprian, Chief Buthelezi and their retinue met me again in Johannesburg and we called on a jeweller named Felix Salm. I had arranged previously for Salm to make me two plain onyx rings, similar to the crested one I

The ailing King Cyprian and his cousin Chief
Gatsha Buthelezi in 1964.

wore myself. I gave one to the king and the other to the chief.
Expressing their gratitude Buthelezi said the rings would serve
not only to keep the three of us bonded in thought, but also to
commemorate the Lion's joyful visit to my surgeon friend.

From Salm's place we drove to my home, KwaVulindlela,
and after lunch spent the rest of the day happily reminiscing in
my research museum. Next morning the king and his party
returned to KwaZulu.

In August I wrote to Buthelezi suggesting that in view of the
king's 'prolonged and disturbing medical history...the Zulu
nation should be informed of his return to health'. It had been

a source of concern to me that gossip-mongers, unaware of his
recent visit to Theron, persisted in spreading false rumours
about his continued enslavement to alcohol. There was even talk
of his impending abdication. The sooner these rumours were
shown to be false, I reasoned, the sooner the minds of 'the rank
and file of KwaZulu, Natal and other Zulu-speaking areas'
would be set at rest. Buthelezi replied that he had also given
thought to the matter, but considered it wiser to wait until after
the king had been re-examined by Mr Theron.

During the three months following his first visit to the
surgeon, King Cyprian conformed in every way to the instructions he had been given. Towards the end of October when he

In Southern Africa some of the most sought after psychics are women. The strings of beads worn by this diviner, V. Khiba, are sewn into the hair

Part of the north-western
section of Lobamba occupied
by the She Elephant's
retainers. The hills in the
background are part of the
sacred Mdzimba range

reported back for examination as arranged, accompanied by Buthelezi, his health was found to have improved beyond even the surgeon's expectations. He had put on weight, but above all he looked more relaxed and contented now than I had ever known him. Pieter Theron in particular was delighted with the progress he had made. However, on our departure he warned the king that should he return to his former ways, he would be courting death.

An hour later I arranged, with the king's consent, for members of the press to meet him. As a result of this interview numbers of newspapers gave prominence to his newly found health. Of all the statements he made, none was as important as the following reported by Carel Birkby in South Africa's *Sunday Times*:

'The King,' he wrote, 'has by his own decision given up alcohol. And in parting he said: "I have a new lease of life. I profoundly hope that this will allow me to help my people for many years."'

When the soul has been clawed and left scarred by alcohol, it tends to fidget and fret and crave for relief. And in craving relief it often grows weak, heedless of the agony that preceded the scars. So it was with King Cyprian.

In January 1965 I learned from Buthelezi that the Lion had been 'seriously ill'. My mind crawled with nagging suspicions. Two months later Buthelezi wrote that the king had recovered, and was, in fact, 'extremely well'. But in May came the news I had dreaded most: the king, wrote Buthelezi, had yielded again to temptation, and was drinking as heavily as he had done in the past. I pleaded in reply that 'something must be done to save him from self-destruction', adding that I 'would be only too pleased to help...' in any way he, Buthelezi, saw fit.

But there was nothing either the chief or I could do for the king. He seemed no longer to want our help. Indeed, during the following eighteen months, although the three of us were to meet on several occasions, the one topic we all avoided was the Lion's reversion to drink.

By September 1966 his health had started to crumble. He had been taken suddenly ill at Khethomthandayo, and was admitted to the Benedictine Mission Hospital, supposedly with a bout of influenza. In December Buthelezi wrote: 'The Ingonyama hasn't been well, and I wonder if you think it possible, say next year, to have him examined again by your esteemed friend, Mr Theron. I think February will be ideal.'

The king's next visit to Theron was not to take place until August 1968, for apparently only then did he realize his life was really in danger, and confess to Buthelezi that he needed help. Following a telephone call from the chief I arranged an appointment for the 23rd, unwittingly the one day Buthelezi could not be present, as there were urgent affairs in KwaZulu that demanded his personal attention.

King Cyprian was brought to Johannesburg by Walter Kanye and we met outside the Medical Centre. Stepping out of his sky-blue Dodge Monaco he looked old, distressed and weak. When he came face to face with Pieter Theron his eyes welled up with tears.

The examination and tests followed exactly the same pattern as on previous occasions, but whereas before the results had brought us joy, now they were to fill us with sorrow. We sat in silence, the king, Kanye and I, waiting for the unhappy verdict we anticipated.

'There's not much I can tell you, King Cyprian, that you don't already know,' Theron began, 'because it would seem you have forgotten the advice I gave you when last you were here, and have failed to keep up the treatment arranged for you at the mission hospital.'

The king lowered his eyes, shakily drawing on a cigarette.

'Your liver condition,' the surgeon continued, 'has worsened considerably, and you have allowed the diabetes to get out of hand. In short, King Cyprian, it pains me to say that unless you co-operate in every way—take the medicines I prescribe for you, report regularly as arranged for treatment at the mission hospital and throw liquor right out of your life, even traditional Zulu beer—you will be dead within a month from today.'

Looking up, his eyes moist and his lips quivering in a faint smile, the Lion nodded pensively. He had heard, he said, and understood.

Parting with Pieter Theron we returned to the Lion's car, parked near the entrance to the Medical Centre. It was surrounded by hundreds of Zulu flat-land workers waiting for their king to appear.

'*Wena weNdlovu! Wena weNdlovu!*—Thou Oh Elephant! *Bayete! Bayete!*' they roared, catching sight of him.

The king paused briefly to acknowledge the royal salute, and then stepped into his car. I sat down beside him on the back seat and, as we inched slowly through the excited throng, I remember gently taking his hand and saying to him:

'*Ingonyama yethu*—Oh, Lion of ours—your people love you. They want you to live. We all want you to live.'

There were tears on his cheeks now. Then suddenly an unwelcome voice whispered within me: 'Does he want to go on living?'

From the Medical Centre we drove to Felix Salm's workshop in Eloff Street. I had learnt during the previous week that the king had lost his onyx ring, so I had had another made for him. This little surprise seemed to brighten his spirits. Later, when

Above The first mourners arrive
on the outskirts of the
Khethomthandayo royal
kraal to attend
King Cyprian's burial.

Five Zulu dignitaries seated
on the floor of the wake
room where the body
of King Cyprian lies
in state. They are,
from left to right,
Prince Samson Zulu,
O.M. Shange,
Prince Clement Zulu,
Chief Gatsha Buthelezi
and Prince Gideon Zulu.

we were about to part, he made a remark which was to linger with me for many days to come:

'Vulindlela,' he said (he always called me by my African name), 'I promise I will never lose this ring; I will wear it forever, even into my grave.'

On Sunday night, 15 September, I received a telephone call from Chief Gatsha Buthelezi. King Cyprian, he said, had collapsed in his car the night before, and had been taken to the mission hospital. Dr George Campbell, a close friend of the Zulu royal house, had been summoned, and on examining the king declared he had not the slightest chance of recovery. Why? Why? I asked Buthelezi. Had the Lion not heeded Pieter Theron's warning? He had not. He had been drinking heavily until the time he climbed into his car for the last time. It seemed that in having to choose between living and dying, he had chosen both.

During the early hours of Tuesday the 17th Buthelezi rang again. Sobbing gently, a clutch in his voice, he told me the king had just died. He, Buthelezi, wanted me to take part in the burial, and would let me know when to come to Khethomthandayo.

I was summoned on the night of the 19th, and setting out next day with my son, Peter, met Buthelezi, his mother Princess Magogo, his wife Irene and his children, in Nongoma, a little before noon on Saturday the 21st. We then drove together to Khethomthandayo.

We passed thousands of Zulu along the route, trudging through the valleys and up the hills—warriors and greybeards, maidens, wives and grandmothers, all clad in traditional dress, all silently heading for the royal kraal. On the crest of the hill where Khethomthandayo stands, we skirted a great village of bell tents specially erected for housing the multitudes streaming in for the burial. Then passing through the gates of the royal kraal our ears were filled with the sound of wailing and weeping. The courtyard swarmed with mourners, many of them paramount chiefs, chiefs, headmen and envoys from neighbouring and distant African territories. But by far the majority were Zulu dignitaries, the menfolk standing together in little groups, and talking in muted tones; the women clothed in black, quietly waiting to enter the late king's home. At the edge of the crowd, weeping convulsively into his hands, was an old man, greybearded and bald.

'*Ngane yami*! *Ngane yami*! My child! My child!' he cried, referring to his departed monarch, 'where will we find another like him?'

On arrival at the front door of King Cyprian's house, we were led by Buthelezi to the room where the Lion lay in state in a glass-topped coffin. There was a cold eeriness about this small, shadowy room. Lining the walls a wake of royal women sat side by side on the floor, their heads and shoulders draped with black mourning shawls, and their whimpers and prayers muffled in the palms of their hands.

My first glimpse into the coffin brought a lump to my throat, for in my mind's eye I saw not King Cyprian's inanimate face of death, but over it the face I had known for fourteen years, now smiling up at me, now tensed with suffering. As slowly the waxen features beneath came into focus, a cold shudder went surging through me. Now for the first time I noticed that the corpse was dressed in the dark blue military uniform the king had so often worn on state occasions. His arms were positioned across his chest and in his hands was a rosary.

We remained in the room for about fifteen minutes. After Buthelezi had presented me to the senior members of the wake, we repaired to the courtyard, where he welcomed the assembly of dignitaries to Khethomthandayo. During the following two hours I found myself in the company of numerous friends whose royal kraals, villages and territories I had visited in years gone by. Then in the early afternoon Buthelezi and I returned to the wake, where I photographed him with the Princes Clement, Gideon and Samson as they knelt beside the coffin.

Meanwhile hundreds of Zulu had lined up outside the royal home waiting for permission to see the corpse. When eventually the doors were opened, they came crawling through the house and into the wake room on hands and knees. Glimpsing into the coffin they crawled out again sobbing and uttering lamentations.

'We have no father,' cried one.

'We have been struck down,' wailed another.

'Who will feed us now?' quavered a third.

Outside the wailing of the crowds rose gradually like the mournful howl of wind in the cliffs, and through it came the strains of a hymn sung by a gathering of women.

Leaving the wake Buthelezi, Prince Samson, my son Peter and I set out by car for Mahashini, Place of Horses, where the grave had been marked out by Prince Peter Dinuzulu, the late king's uncle. Arriving on the outskirts of Dlamahlahla, formerly King Solomon's royal kraal, we came upon thousands of Zulu warriors already gathered for the burial. The sun was setting now, and they were collecting firewood for the evening meal, or putting the final touches to makeshift shelters they had built from branches chopped in the bush. We visited the grave site, had discussions with the dignitaries resident at Mahashini, and then, with darkness crowding in, returned to Nongoma.

Early next morning, having spent the night at the small hotel in the village, I reported to Buthelezi at Khethomthandayo. I found him in conversation with the royal relatives selected to head the great procession of cars to Mahashini. It was then I learned that I was to drive three of the king's younger children to the burial place—the Princesses Nolindi and Mbonisi, and the eleven-year-old Prince Mduduzi.

At about ten o'clock the royal corpse was moved from the wake room and placed in a hearse parked in the courtyard. Then the cortège, headed by a squad of the Zulu royal guards clad in khaki uniforms, crept slowly towards the main gates. Entering the dusty road beyond, and proceeding past the tent encampment, some two hundred and fifty cars fell in behind us. The first two kilometres of the route were lined on either side by thousands of Zulu, their tremulous cries accompanying the hearse as it threaded its way down the hill.

Later in my diary I described the scene as follows:

'Here and there I could see Zulu women kneeling in the grass, some turning moist, screwed-up faces to the sky, others loudly praying with hands clasped before them. The older men wept bitterly and unashamedly, the younger more discreetly, while the children stared wide-eyed, now at the funeral procession and now at their lamenting elders. To the left and the right of us herdboys came capering across the veld to meet the procession, but confronted suddenly by the hearse, they halted, huddled together and gazed wide-eyed at the coffin as it glided past.'

The road to Mahashini meanders through a succession of mountain passes, and as the line of cars snaked slowly westwards, the valleys withdrew into a haze of dust.

'The clouds of fine-powdered dust kicked up from the road were so dense that the cars fore and aft appeared and disappeared like phantoms in an eerie mist. It was not surprising therefore that the fourteen-kilometre drive to Mahashini should have taken us almost two hours.'

The diary continues: 'About a mile from the burial place two streams of mourners, walking four to six abreast, followed the road on either side. Approaching the burial site I could see fleets of buses, a great mosaic of cars parked in the veld and a multitude of people bound for Dlamahlahla.

'On arrival at the north-eastern side of the woods outside Mahashini, the hearse and chief mourners' cars were quickly encircled by a crowd of Zulu jostling and straining for a glimpse at the coffin…and when it (the coffin) had been taken down by the pall-bearers, namely the sons of King Solomon, Clement, Barold and Samson, and the Princes Isiah KaMshiyeni, Gideon KaMnyayiza and Layton KaBabana Zulu, a platoon of policemen came forward and opened a pathway for us to the grave. An estimated forty thousand Zulu, together with a handful of whites, had already assembled at the site. Even the topmost branches of the trees swarmed with tribesmen determined not to miss a moment of the impending two-hour ceremony.'

The coffin was placed on a narrow table beside the grave. It was covered with lion and leopard skins, and on either side stood two tall candles, their flames rigid like assegai blades in the hot, stagnant air. Overlooking both coffin and grave was a platform on which sat the Rt Rev Alpheus Zulu, Anglican bishop of KwaZulu, several ministers of various denominations, J. J. Boshoff, commissioner-general of KwaZulu, Senator R. Cadman, Chief Gatsha Buthelezi and other well-known personalities.

Soon after our arrival Buthelezi called the crowds to attention. Then followed a long succession of eulogies delivered by chosen speakers, both black and white. Many wonderful things were said, but nothing as moving as the final tribute to the deceased Lion, delivered by Buthelezi himself. His voice trembling, he recalled the long history of suffering King Cyprian had endured, and, among other things, expressed anger at the rumours currently spread by mischief-makers that the king had died as a result of sorcery. There had been no such thing! he cried. He, Buthelezi, and others present were in possession of written evidence received from the country's most eminent doctors to prove that death had followed a prolonged history of diabetes.

After the eulogies, hymns were sung and prayers said, and in due course the coffin was lowered into the grave, a huge rectangular hole roughly seven paces in length, four across and four metres deep. Then the royal regiments began chanting ancient traditional dirges, and led by Buthelezi the forty thousand mourners bellowed repeatedly:

'*Wena weNdlovu! Wena weNdlovu!* Thou Oh Elephant!—*Bayete!*'

Meanwhile members of the royal house had gathered around the grave, and taking earth from a heap nearby dropped it on to the coffin.

Gradually the crowd began to disperse. King Nyangayezizwe Cyprian Bhekuzulu, son of King Nkayishana Solomon Maphumzana, had 'gone home' forever.

Ceremony at KwaVulindlela

After the death of King Cyprian, his son, the twenty-year-old Prince Zwelithini, What Does the World Have to Say? was proclaimed the future king of the Zulu, but as he was considered too young to rule, his uncle, Prince Mcwayizeni, was appointed to act as regent for an indefinite period. I had never met Prince Zwelithini—he had always been away at school when I visited his father—and had met the regent only twice. My direct contact with the Zulu royal house therefore came abruptly to an end. In any case, learning that Chief Gatsha Buthelezi and Prince Mcwayizeni had recently clashed over matters concerning the royal house, and were said to have become estranged, I believed it expedient to keep away from Khethomthandayo.

Weeping mourners fling
themselves on to the
ground at the graveside,
King Cyprian's coffin
now draped with lion
and leopard skins.

Prince Mcwayizeni Israel Zulu
appointed regent of the
Zulu nation after
King Cyprian's death.

In June, following an election in KwaZulu, Buthelezi became the first chief executive officer, or prime minister, of the Zulu Territorial Authority. A month later I was invited to Prince Zwelithini's twenty-first birthday celebration at Nxangiphilile, home of the regent Prince Mcwayizeni. To my great disappointment the invitation card arrived while I was on an expedition in the Kalahari desert, and my family was unable to contact me. I received comfort, however, from a premonition I had had that the future king would soon come into my life in an unexpected way.

On the morning of 22 October 1969, a little more than a year since King Cyprian's last visit to Pieter Theron, I received a telephone call from Princess Morjinah, Buthelezi's sister, then resident in Daveyton near Benoni. Prince Nelson Shamase, the late king's brother-in-law, she told me, had arrived at her home accompanied by Prince Zwelithini and a small retinue of princes. They had an important matter to discuss with me, and wanted to know how soon I could see them?

I arranged with the princess for the royal party to be brought to my office in Johannesburg during the afternoon. About ten minutes before they were due to arrive, whilst pondering the purpose of the visit, it occurred to me that I should prepare something special to say to the heir-apparent when once the meeting was over. One of the thoughts that came to mind I wrote on my desk pad in Zulu as follows:

'Young Lion-to-be, son of King Nyangayezizwe Cyprian Bhekuzulu, I counted your father among my dearest friends. Therefore, if I should be granted a wish, it would be that I be given the right to look upon you as my son, and become as close to you as I am to my own two sons.'

On second thoughts I decided against preconditioning myself for Prince Zwelithini's visit, and to allow my remarks to be inspired by what emerged from the impending interview. I therefore tossed the pad aside.

When the royal party arrived and I was introduced to the young prince, I conceived an instant liking for him. He looked startlingly like his father, and his laugh had the same heartiness that had endeared King Cyprian to friends and subjects, and of course to me.

During the following half hour we drank tea, smoked and exchanged pinches of snuff. And we talked of the illness, death and burial of the former king, whose photograph, incidentally, smiled down at us from among many others of African rulers displayed on my office walls. Then suddenly Nelson Shamase came to the point.

The Zulu royal house, and to a great extent the nation as a whole, he said, had long been aware of the close association I had enjoyed with the late King Cyprian. Therefore, as spokesman of the royal party he, Shamase, had a favour to ask me: would I accept Prince Zwelithini, the future Lion, as my son, to guide and advise him as his father-guardian? This was in line with age-old custom, he added, except of course that I was a white man, and in addition not born of the Zulu royal house. But would I accept, Shamase repeated, if for no other reason than because it would have been the late Lion's wish?

I was thunderstruck! My mind flashed to the words I had written before their arrival. So, reaching for the pad, I gave it to Shamase to read to the rest of the party. They all burst into laughter, clapping their hands. Was this not a sign, cried Nelson Shamase, that the party's mission to Johannesburg had been spiritually inspired?

Of course I would gladly accept the honour, I replied. There was more clapping now. Then waiting for silence I continued:

'This is not a favour I shall be doing you, but a privilege you are bestowing upon me. And as is the custom in a case such as this, I, the recipient, must *hlabisa* (slaughter a beast) so that we can feast and commemorate what promises to be one of the happiest days of my life.

'But I have a problem,' I said, switching to Zulu metaphor, 'my cattle are away in the hills, and I ask to be allowed a day or two in order to have them brought back to my "kraal", Kwa-Vulindlela, in Bryanston.'

'This we agree to,' replied Shamase, 'so we will return to you a week from today. We too want to prepare for the ceremony.'

Whereupon the royal party departed leaving me alone with my thoughts.

Next day I telephoned Princess Morjinah only to learn that Shamase, Prince Zwelithini and the retinue had returned to KwaZulu. She assured me they would be back on the appointed day, and advised me, tongue in cheek, not to delay fetching my cattle from the hills. That evening Buthelezi rang me from his royal residence, KwaPhindangene. He had been delighted to hear the news. The spirit of King Cyprian, he said, must be smiling and nodding its head in approval.

On the morning of Thursday the 29th the royal party, headed again by Prince Nelson Shamase, arrived at my office as arranged. On this occasion the party consisted of twenty-two men including Prince Matthews Zulu, the late king's 'funny man', four other princes of the Zulu royal house, and *Induna* (commander) Mhleko and the royal *imbongi* or praise-singer, Gexezile Zulu. Unlike the rest of the party, who were formally dressed in European clothes, he wore a leopard-skin headdress and a kilt of genet tails, and he carried a battle-axe, its blade shaped like the wings of a swallow in flight. After exchanging greetings we departed for KwaVulindlela, I leading the convoy of cars.

Prince Zwelithini KaBhekuzulu,
heir-apparent to the
Zulu throne.

Induna Mhleko, Zulu regimental commander.

KwaVulindlela lies at the foot of a chain of wooded and rock-crested hills overlooking the beautiful valleys of Bryanston. As the homes in the vicinity lie far apart, and are tucked away in a generous growth of indigenous bush and tree, I saw my 'kraal' as the ideal spot for a ceremony of so private a nature. But there was to be nothing private about the arrival of the Zulu at KwaVulindlela. Bugles blowing, voices combined in singing and chanting, and the *imbongi*'s bellowings, all so strange to the surroundings as to send doves, sparrows, finches, barbets and plovers catapulting into the sky. My children's horses went on a galloping spree round the paddock, and their dogs were so bewildered that they bounded away, some to seek sanctuary in the shrubberies, and others indoors. In what seemed like minutes the lawns thronged with local Africans—Pedi-, Tswana- and Shangana-speaking. And this, I had hoped, would be a private affair!

The ceremony itself was held in the quiet of my research museum. Apart from the royal party and myself, it was witnessed only by six others—my sons, Harold and Peter, my little girls, Nandi and Lindi, Joe Openshaw, a staff reporter of *The Star* and finally his photographer.

How does one describe a ceremony so personal, so sincere and so gratifying, when the one honoured was, indeed, oneself? Now as I write I am confronted with an insubordination of words, albeit every second of the lengthy proceedings was recorded on tape. Let it be enough to say that Nelson Shamase, Prince Matthews and the princes took turns in recalling events that had brought me into contact with the Zulu royal house. Not only as a friend of King Cyprian, but, according to one of the speakers, as 'the one whose books had brought to life, and into true perspective, the Zulu nation's proudest heroes'.

'It was history being made in Bryanston,' wrote Openshaw next day in *The Star*, 'a moving and dignified ceremony...the Prince (Zwelithini)...sitting on a chair covered with a leopard skin; a mark of respect to royalty. The Princes, *indunas* and re-tainers sat on animal pelts in traditional fashion. Many times during the oratory and peaens of praise, the oxhide shields and drums resounded to the royal salute of "*Wena we Ndlovu! Wena we Ndlovu! Bayete! Bayete!*"

'Prince Nelson was the first to speak: "Your friendship to King Cyprian and the Zulu nation," he said to Dr Becker, "is a very great thing; it is like young love and something that cannot be stopped. We accept you as father of the Prince. We wish you long life so that you can give guidance to your son in the ways of modern life."'

Describing the closing phases of the ceremony, Openshaw continued:

'Dr Becker replied [to the various speakers] in Zulu and English. The men of the Royal Kraal sat in statuesque attention. "I have travelled and researched among all Black people of Southern Africa," he said. "I have seen much, but the greatest honour has come to me now. I am father to the future King of the Zulu. My heart is full of happiness. You, Zwelithini, are my son. Therefore Zwelithini KaBhekuzulu take my hands and live long and well," and he placed an onyx ring on the Prince's finger.'

The ring, I told Zwelithini, was like the one that my ancestors had worn, that my eldest son and I were wearing now, and that I had given King Cyprian and Chief Gatsha Buthelezi to wear.

The last speaker was the future king himself. His heart, he said, was as full of joy as his new father, Vulindlela, had claimed his heart to be. As a son he would expect his new father not only to advise and steer him into paths of wisdom, but also to correct him should he, Zwelithini, step out of line.

'Now I am in my own home right here at KwaVulindlela,' he concluded, 'and when I visit you again, my father, I will come knowing that this is truly my father's home.'

In the final paragraph of his article Openshaw wrote: 'When the ceremony was over it left the feeling that there are ways of getting to the hearts of men who are from different cultures and of different colour—the way of mutual trust and giving.'

When twenty-two men share, as they did that day at Kwa-Vulindlela, a meal of fourteen roasted chickens, a variety of Zulu dishes and an abundance of traditional sorghum beer, then their hearts, however happy, suddenly become happier still. Add to this the antics of a man as comical as the 'royal jester', Prince Matthews Zulu, and the conviviality of the occasion becomes indelibly printed on the minds of everyone present. As Prince Shamase put it: 'In years to come when all of us are greybearded and withered with age, we will look back with nostalgia on those wonderful hours enjoyed at KwaVulindlela.'

The Coronation of King Zwelithini

Two months after his visit to KwaVulindlela, Prince Zwelithini married Sibongile, We are Thankful, daughter of Thomas Dlamini of Njangempela in the Nongoma district. The cere-mony was conducted by Bishop Alpheus Zulu at the St Margaret's Anglican church in the village and the reception took place at Khethomthandayo.

In August 1971 I was informed by the Zulu royal house that Prince Zwelithini was to be crowned king on Friday 3 December. During the following month a letter arrived from Chief Gatsha Buthelezi signed in his capacity as chief executive officer of the Zulu Territorial Authority.

'As a friend of the late King of the Zulu, Ingonyama

Queen Sibongile,
Prince Zwelithini's
senior wife.

Nyangayezizwe Cyprian Bhekuzulu,' it read, 'and as my friend and as a friend of the Zulu nation, I wish to appeal to you to use your best influence to get us the utmost assistance for the installation of Prince Zwelithini KaBhekuzulu.

'I leave it to your wisdom to decide the form which such assistance could take. I have however the following in mind apart from the catering side:

'A chair or throne for the Zulu king, with perhaps the carved coat of arms of the Zulu royal house, and the carved heads of lions on either side. Also a sceptre, which should be in the form of an up-turned battle-axe (*inhlendla*); a leopardskin cloak or cape which could be draped across the shoulders; some kind of golden *isicoco* (headring) or a gold-coated one, and a large canopy that can be held over the throne.'

A week later Buthelezi telephoned to say he had arrived in Johannesburg bound for Europe, and had an urgent matter concerning the coronation to discuss with me. We arranged to meet in my office.

For almost an entire day we planned an elaborate coronation brochure based on notes he had made in consultation with Prince Zwelithini and the Zulu royal council. At his request I undertook to have it professionally designed, printed in Johannesburg and delivered to Khethomthandayo by the end of November. It was to include not only a detailed programme, but also a concise biography of each of the Zulu kings and regents since the time of Shaka, together with appropriate illustrations. I promised that the moment a draft had been done, I would send copies to P.H. (Henry) Torlage, the new KwaZulu commissioner-general, Nils A. Otte, Bantu affairs commissioner in Nongoma, the regent, Prince Mcwayizeni, and Bishop Alpheus Zulu. I also undertook to negotiate with Southern Africa's largest brewery for a donation of beer. Should this be granted I was to arrange delivery to Khethomthandayo on the eve of the coronation. Two days later Buthelezi left for London by aeroplane.

I set to work without delay, and within a fortnight had had the brochure designed, and copies of the draft sent off by post as agreed. I had also summoned the aid of three influential friends, Alf Leveson, Peter Fox and Leslie Richfield, and as if with the touch of the legendary Midas they found sponsors for the various items required for the coronation—the throne, sceptre, leopardskin cloak, headring and canopy. And the brewery promised to have a truckload of beer, spirits and mineral waters delivered to Khethomthandayo by 2 December. There seemed little more for me to do but wait for all these items to be made and brought to my home.

In October I received a reply from Nils Otte in response to the draft I had sent him. Expressing thanks for the trouble I had taken, he tactfully added that the brochure had come as a surprise 'since a programme had already been prepared, using a draft made by Buthelezi' and delivered to the commissioner's office by Prince Zwelithini himself. The prince, he continued, although not in agreement with the version I had sent, was nevertheless delighted to learn I had undertaken to see to the printing. Attached to the letter was a copy of the official programme for my information.

What was I to do? It was not my prerogative, I told myself, to inform Buthelezi that this programme barely resembled the one we had worked on together. I had no choice but to have a new design made and then to proceed with the printing.

The first of the other items to reach me was Prince Zwelithini's cloak. It was made of two leopard skins, the heads facing each other across the chest, and the legs and tails hanging loosely at the sides. Next came the sceptre, then the golden headring, and finally the canopy, delicately fashioned in purple velvet, edged with golden tassels and embossed with the coat of arms of the royal house. During the last week in November the throne arrived, and was presented to Ezikiah Buthelezi, Chief Gatsha's uncle. Arrangements were then made for it to be delivered to Embelebeleni, home of a prince called Sithela Zulu, in Durban's KwaMashu township. The prince in turn was to send it by truck to Khethomthandayo. The huge consignment of programmes printed in Zulu, Afrikaans and English arrived at my home at about the same time. This, together with the canopy, was collected by Dr Dotwana of Daveyton, Princess Morjinah's husband, for delivery to Khethomthandayo. I myself had only the leopardskin cloak, the sceptre and the headring to take. As things turned out this was a most convenient arrangement, for my wife and daughters were accompanying me not only to the coronation, but also thereafter to the Western Cape Province where I had arranged some months before to do research. What with the family luggage and my gear and camera equipment there was barely room left in my car for a stowaway mouse.

Meanwhile, according to newspaper reports throughout the country, KwaZulu seethed with rumours of a bitter clash between Prince Zwelithini and his councillors on the one hand and Buthelezi, now back from Europe, on the other. Buthelezi's life was said to have been threatened by anonymous enemies outside the royal house, and he was further reported to be attending the coronation under escort of a bodyguard. Even I was reputed to have become estranged from the Zulu royal house, and according to one of the papers was bound to be cold-shouldered on arrival at Khethomthandayo.

At dawn on Thursday 2 December, we set out for Nongoma amidst a cannonade of thunder and lightning and the drumming of rain. During the past week the entire country had been relentlessly drenched, and according to reports Kwa-

Zulu had been blasted by the severest storms in twenty-five years.

Crossing the flooded Pongolo river just after midday, we sluiced into the narrow dirt road that curls through the hills and bush to Nongoma, seventy-six kilometres ahead. In 1968, on my return home from King Cyprian's burial, this road had been obscured in dust. Now it was sodden and deep in mud. We reached Nongoma at 3.30 p.m.

After a brief interview with members of a BBC television team, local radio men and a squad of newspaper reporters in the yard outside the commissioner's offices, I took my family to the home of friends who, having learned that the local hotel was bursting at the seams with government officials attending the coronation, had invited us to stay with them in Nongoma.

Returning to the commissioner's offices half an hour later, I found Chief Gatsha Buthelezi awaiting me. We left immediately for Khethomthandayo, having arranged to meet Prince Zwelithini at 5 p.m. The rain had lifted now, but driving through mist and slush ploughed deep by countless cars that crept with us across the hills we entered the royal kraal about twenty minutes before the appointed time. On enquiry we learned that the young prince had left Khethomthandayo with a retinue an hour before, and had not said when he was likely to return. A little crestfallen, I wondered whether he had decided to snub us after all, as had been predicted two days before.

Buthelezi and I repaired to the late King Cyprian's house—a new home had been built for the future king about a hundred metres away—and there we waited. We were met in the living room by members of the royal family, among whom was Princess Magogo, Buthelezi's mother. I could sense that Buthelezi was offended at the prince's absence. Fingers crossed, I decided to leave impending events to Providence.

About half an hour later Prince Zwelithini arrived by car at the gates of Khethomthandayo, and followed by the retinue strode down the road leading from the gates to his home. Then came a message that the prince was ready to see us, delivered by O. M. Mdengentonga (Although Short My Deeds are Great) Shange, African commissioner of the Natal Boy Scouts, and friend of the Zulu royal house.

So, fetching the leopardskin cloak, the sceptre, the golden headring and three cameras from my car, we headed for the future king's home.

We found Prince Zwelithini seated in an arm chair, nonchalantly puffing at a cigarette. Pausing at the door we raised our right hands, cried '*Bayete!*', and entered. We were joined a few moments later by Prince Peter Dinuzulu, the Princesses Magogo, Morjinah and others, and we all sat down in a wide circle facing Prince Zwelithini. An uneasy silence now fell over the little gathering, so I padded across the room and settled in a chair left vacant beside the future Lion. During the next few minutes we conversed in whispers, he and I, recalling the happy day when he was brought to KwaVulindlela to be made my son, and I his father.

Then into the room crawled a most welcome visitor, an infant boy who I correctly guessed was Lethukuthula, Bringer of Peace, Prince Zwelithini's son and future heir to the Zulu throne. And now, as we watched him struggle to unwrap the three gifts I had brought, we all laughed together. Whatever tensions there might have been some moments before drifted away. Suddenly there seemed a great deal to talk about, and much to enjoy in each other's company.

After tea had been served I presented the gifts to Prince Zwelithini, explaining that they had been inspired by Buthelezi and arranged by me through friends of mine. He immediately put on the leopardskin cloak, and with feigned conceit asked me to take his photograph. He then had the purple canopy fetched and erected in the centre of the room, and the throne placed beneath it. For almost an hour I photographed him in various poses, first on his own, then with the queen, and lastly in the company of the princes and, of course, the tiny Bringer of Peace, Lethukuthula.

Buthelezi and I eventually left just after nine o'clock, and driving back to Nongoma we agreed that the evening's conviviality had augured well for the coronation.

Friday the 3rd dawned in drizzle and mist, and there was a chill in the wind which even seemed to make the village roosters crow off key. There could not have been a more inauspicious beginning to this important day. After gulping down a cup of coffee we set out for Khethomthandayo. Slithering through the hills we wondered if the coronation would in fact take place, but concluded, knowing the determination of the Zulu people, that they would allow neither rain, nor wind, nor even a blizzard to intervene.

About a kilometre south-west of the royal kraal an immense amphitheatre had been carved out of the side of a hill by the Natal and KwaZulu Works Department. It was here that the coronation was to be held. On arrival at the site we found it sheeted with waters cascading down from the surrounding slopes. Along the bottom edge of the arena, hazed in mists, were two mammoth plastic tents patterned with broad stripes, yellow and green. Containing many hundreds of seats reserved for honoured guests, they flapped and jerked and groaned in the wind, and in places they leaned precariously to the south as if poised to take off in flight across the valleys. Like sailors of bygone days, heaving at the lanyards of a storm-swept schooner,

Prince Zwelithini on the eve of his coronation.

A section of the multitudes who attended Prince Zwelithini's coronation.

Warriors and tribesmen mingle in the muddy
amphitheatre built for the coronation at
Nongoma.

A Zulu regimental bugler waits for the sign to call the warriors to order.

King Zwelithini, newly crowned
Ingonyama or Lion of the
Zulu nation.

teams of Zulu tugged at the ropes striving to straighten and steady the tents. Then gradually the wind began to drop and the drizzle to soften. At last there was hope that the skies might be kind to Prince Zwelithini.

By eight o'clock the rain had stopped and thousands of Zulu spectators had begun occupying the terraced slopes above us. An hour later the chiefs of KwaZulu entered and crossed the arena, taking up places to the right of the dais where the king would be seated during the ceremony. They were followed by government officials and invited guests, among them Prince Makhosini Dlamini, prime minister of Swaziland, and his party, exquisitely dressed in traditional regalia. Next came Buthelezi attired in feathers and skins in the fashion of the conqueror, Shaka. He was followed by Bishop Alpheus Zulu and he in turn by Prince Zwelithini himself, Queen Sibongile, the regent, Mcwayizeni, Walter Kanye and members of the royal house headed by Shange and the Zulu boy scouts. At eleven o'clock the Hon. M. C. Botha, MP and Minister of Bantu Administration and Development, arrived accompanied by his wife, Commissioner-General Torlage and his wife, Bantu Affairs Commissioner Otte with his wife, and others.

By this time the arena swarmed with Zulu regiments, invited guests, press reporters and photographers, television and newsreel cameramen and scores of guards and policemen. I myself had a front row seat between the veteran anthropologist, Dr Eileen Krige, and Dr George Campbell, who had examined King Cyprian on the eve of his death. There was tumult around us—the drone of thousands of voices, the chanting of warriors and the blare of a military band. Then the gathering was called to order, and the proceedings opened in prayer led by the bishop of KwaZulu.

Meanwhile the rain had returned and a faint mist oozed over the crowds. During the following two hours speeches were delivered in turn by the regent, Nils Otte, Henry Torlage, and M. C. Botha, the minister, who also presented Prince Zwelithini with official letters of appointment. Finally the gathering was addressed by the newly installed king himself. Many of the spectators had thought he would be 'crowned' in European style by Bishop Alpheus Zulu, knowing this to be the wish of certain influential members of the Zulu hierarchy. However, as the idea had been rejected by the royal house, declaring it foreign to Zulu protocol, the golden *isicoco* (headring) had been left behind at Khethomthandayo. Whilst the new king spoke the crowds, most of them drenched and chilled to the marrow, listened in silence. And from time to time, when he referred to the late King Cyprian, or to other ancestral kings, they bellowed the royal salute, '*Bayete!*', as if they intended all the world to hear. At one stage of his address, recalling the suffering his father

had endured against the odds of fast-failing health, the young king broke down and wept. A low murmur of compassion pervaded the amphitheatre, until suddenly the warriors, holding their shields and assegais aloft cried out: '*Wena weNdlovu! Wena weNdlovu!* Thou Oh Elephant! *Bayete!*'

The drizzle had died away by the time King Zwelithini had completed his speech. Swaggering into the arena he signalled the regiments to dance. This was a magnificent sight, and, as the ground squelched with the stomping of warrior feet, the eyes of the spectators fell suddenly on Chief Gatsha Buthelezi. Shield and swallow-wing battle-axe in hand, his headdress of *sakabuli* ('long-tailed widow bird') feathers undulating in the breeze, he came loping forward amidst a roar of acclamation to join in the dance.

When the dancing ended the king and his retinue, the minister and government officials, and the chiefs and other dignitaries left the arena in cars and jeeps, and the crowd began to disperse. Ironically the sun now came filtering through a patch of haze. Out-manoeuvred so far by the leaden skies, it was soon to command full view of events to follow, and a ritual as rare and spectacular as any the Zulu themselves had witnessed before.

Bull-Killing Ceremony

I remained in the arena for about an hour, meeting old friends including Francis Mncube, then the mayor of Soweto, Johannesburg's urban African complex, Peter Lengene, who was later to succeed him, Bishop Alpheus Zulu and Walter Kanye. It was then that a feature writer of *The Star* drew me aside, and asked if I would use my influence with the king to have him admitted to the Bull-Killing ceremony, due to take place on the following day in the royal cattlefold at Khethomthandayo. I explained to him that I had discreetly avoided discussing the event with members of the royal house, let alone the Lion. The Zulu royal council had decreed against permitting white men to attend this part of the coronation. Moreover, I had learnt that a large area embracing the cattlefold was to be cordoned off by the South African police.

'You are wrong,' he replied, 'because I was told this morning by a senior member of the royal house that you, Torlage, Otte, Eileen Krige and Aubrey Elliott of Pretoria would be invited to attend. On the strength of this I thought the king might let me in.'

My heart turned a somersault. I had privately prayed that I might be afforded this wonderful privilege, realizing, of course, that unless invited by King Zwelithini himself I had no hope of being admitted to the cattlefold. There was nothing I could do but wait for a call that might never come.

Prince Makhosini Dlamini (centre) Prime
Minister of Swaziland and leader of the
Swazi party at King Zwelithini's coronation.
The Zulu dignitary with the shield is Chief
Gatsha Buthelezi.

Some of the thousands of Zulu warriors who
gathered at Khethomthandayo to pay homage
to their newly-crowned Lion.

According to present-day Zulu chroniclers and the journals written by the earliest white pioneers during their visits to KwaZulu, the Bull-Killing ceremony was widely practised among East Coast Nguni clans in olden times, as indeed it is practised annually to this day in Swaziland. It had formed part of the *Umkhosi* or Zulu First-Fruits ceremony, but by the turn of the nineteenth century it had been abandoned in most parts of KwaZulu. As far as can be ascertained it had never been observed by the Zulu clan, either before or during the rule of Chief Senzangakhona.

At the time of King Shaka's rise to power, the most ardent adherents to this ancient ritual were the Ndwandwe, Mthethwa, Qwabe, Shezi, Mhlongo and Mkhize clans. Determined to introduce uniformity to his newly founded Zulu empire, King Shaka, Senzangakhona's successor, had ruled that the *Umkhosi* be held only at Bulawayo, his first military kraal, and then later only at Gibixhegu, which he built in 1820 near present-day Empangeni. Vassal chiefs had therefore to forfeit the right to conduct their own Bull-Killing ceremonies. In the years to follow it became customary for the bull, symbol of fertility and virility, to be slain not only during the *Umkhosi* celebrations, but also at the inauguration of the royal regiments and the coronation of Zulu kings.

In more recent times the Bull-Killing ceremony, often referred to colloquially as *ukushwema* or *ukunqaka* or *ukuphahleka uswella*, was to be resuscitated by some of the clans—the Nyuswa of the Ndwedwe and Pietermaritzburg districts, the Ndwandwe and the Gumede of Hlabisa—as an annual event. In 1948 it had formed the climax of King Cyprian's coronation, just as it was to be at the coronation of Zwelithini on the afternoon of Saturday 4 December 1971.

Towards evening on Friday the 3rd I received a message from the new king to come to Khethomthandayo on the following morning. He wanted me to take photographs for the royal house of events due to start at ten o'clock. No mention was made of the Bull-Killing ceremony.

Arriving next day at the main gates under clear skies and a broiling sun, I was met by Prince Nelson Shamase and Mdengentonga Shange, the Short Man Renowned for his Deeds. The three of us, laden with my cameras and photographic equipment, then elbowed a way through a multitude of Africans gathered in a great semi-circle in front of the king's home. Entering an open space ringed by the crowds, I caught sight of the king on the opposite side. He was seated on the throne I had had made for him, and was shaded from the slanting rays of the morning sun by the purple canopy, held erect by four royal guards.

To the right of the king sat Henry Torlage the commissioner-general, Nils Otte, Francis Mncube and a number of chieftains draped in leopardskin cloaks. On his left was Prince Makhosini Dlamini, prime minister of Swaziland, the Swazi regimental commander, Induna Ngangenyoni Twala, and other important Swazi visitors. I had barely reached the throne to greet the king when two Zulu regiments came charging into the open space. Suddenly Khethomthandayo resounded to the chanting of the warriors, the clatter of their fighting sticks, the thud of shields being struck on the ground, the trilling of platoons of women dressed in traditional finery and the tumultuous cheering of the crowds.

'*Wena we Ndlovu! Wena we Ndlovu! Bayete!*', roared the throng, and all around us the earth seemed to shudder beneath the dancing of the warriors, their feet now rising, now crashing to the ground with a hollow thud.

After the regiments had danced before their new Lion a party of chieftains arrived. Presenting the king with a white stallion, saddled and bridled, they took turns in wishing him well. Then came a group of royal women bearing among other gifts a magnificent kaross made of jackal and springbok pelts. During the remainder of the morning King Zwelithini and his guests were entertained to a programme of exotic dancing, choral singing and acrobatics performed by troupes of urban Zulu from as far afield as Durban, Johannesburg and Welkom. There was also a march past of Shange's Zulu boy scouts, and a parade of prancing, strutting, high-stepping teenage drum-majorettes, all trimly fitted out in satin frocks of red and purple, white knee-high boots and peaked caps fronted with ostrich feathers. Then the regiments began dancing again, to the accompaniment of their singing and chanting of battle cries. One by one, and occasionally in pairs, the warriors came loping out of the ranks, flinging themselves wildly into a display of mock combat—parrying, ducking, stabbing, colliding, falling. Meanwhile I had been at work with my cameras in the open space, dodging the various performers, and on occasions almost trodden under foot by the regiments.

At about 1.30 p.m. I noticed that my cameras needed reloading, so I retired to the side of the king's house, where I had left the rest of my equipment in the care of a Zulu guard.

No sooner had I reached the spot than a window opened, and glancing up, I beheld King Zwelithini smiling down at me.

'*Baba*, my father,' he whispered in Zulu, 'you must go at once to the cattlefold. I will send men to help you carry your cameras.'

With that he disappeared from view, shutting the window behind him. Now for the first time I knew for certain I would be witnessing the Bull-Killing ceremony. What thrilled me most was the thought that, unlike King Sobhuza of Swaziland, King Zwelithini wanted the ritual photographed.

King Zwelithini watches
regimental dancing
on the day after his
coronation. Seated on his
right is the Commissioner
General of KwaZulu,
Mr Henry Torlage.

Five minutes later I found Prince Clement Zulu at my side, accompanied by Shange and a royal guard named George Mlambo. The king, he said, had arranged for Henry Torlage, Nils Otte, Eileen Krige, Aubrey Elliott and myself to be taken under escort to the cattlefold. I would find them waiting for me beside the throne, so I must join them immediately with Shange and Mlambo, who would help me carry my equipment.

Reaching the throne two minutes later Shange, Mlambo and I discovered to our dismay that the rest of the party had already left, so we decided to sit down in the shade of the canopy and wait for the king to appear.

Meanwhile seven regiments (the Vukayibambe, Nqabayembube, Phondolwendlovu, Ntabayezulu, Manukelana, Khiphinkunzi and Mkhuphulangwenya) had formed up in marching order, eight warriors abreast, and when the Lion stepped out of his home, signalling them to follow, they surged forward roaring the royal salute. So we jumped to our feet, I with three cameras hanging from my neck, and Shange and Mlambo with haversacks strapped to their backs containing an assortment of film and lenses. We kept about five paces ahead of the noisy procession, for fear of being left behind and not knowing what else to do. Then, moving through the main gates of the royal kraal, we were stopped by a colonel of the South African police, who declared he had been given orders to keep white spectators away from the cattlefold and had therefore to turn me back. By this time the procession of regiments had veered away to the left, leaving us to remonstrate with the stern-faced colonel. It seemed after all that I would not be witnessing the Bull-Killing ceremony.

After explaining my predicament, and pleading with him, the colonel sent a sergeant to enquire from Torlage and Otte if I had in fact been invited to the Bull-Killing ceremony. Three long minutes later the sergeant returned. He had been told to bring me to the cattlefold without further delay. So Shange, Mlambo and I were quickly led across the veld to where Torlage and the rest of the party awaited me. But we found them outside the cattlefold viewing the interior through slits in the encircling palisade, and thronged with Zulu men of all ages and sizes. I could see at a glance that if I joined them I would find it impossible to photograph the ceremony, as the young king had asked me to do.

'Come,' said Mlambo, a little agitated now by the turn of events, 'you must follow me. I was given instructions by the Lion to take you into the cattlefold, and if I fail to do so he will be angry.'

So, thanking the sergeant for the help he had given us, we took a circuitous route round the milling crowds to the opposite side of the cattlefold where the gates were situated. On arrival we found the regiments pressed tightly together, waiting impatiently for the signal to enter. Bracing himself as if poised for an assault on some impregnable fortress, Mlambo now began shouldering a way into the wall of warriors, beckoning Shange and me to follow. We were bumped, jostled and cursed as we inched ahead through the sweaty bodies. Indeed, the crush was so great that I was sometimes lifted high off the ground, my feet walking on air.

In the intense heat and humidity I could scarcely breathe and the pulse in my temples beat noisily. After a five minute struggle we broke through to the front line of the mob and were rudely pushed into the cattlefold. Not three paces away stood King Zwelithini, resplendent in his traditional kingly regalia, and as he gave me a welcoming smile I seemed to myself more like the legendary prodigal son than like a Zulu Lion's father-guardian.

It will be recalled that the royal cattlefold at Khethomthandayo had been built for King Cyprian in 1948. In the course of twenty-three years, therefore, the floor had become deep in cowdung, and now after the recent rains, while it baked in the heat of the sun, it resembled a steaming bog.

No sooner had I arrived than King Zwelithini, flanked by princes, chiefs, and regimental commanders, moved forward, skirting the inner edge of the palisades. Striding backwards I photographed the procession until it had formed a circle around the interior of the cattlefold. In the centre, knee deep in dung, was a small herd of heifers, like the one I had seen at Lobamba in Swaziland, and in its midst was the bull. Led by the king, the former regent, Prince Mcwayizeni, and the *indunas* Mhleko and Cebekhulu, the regiments now began to sing. Then came a party of braves through the gates, and lined up close by to wait for a signal from the king to attack and destroy the bull.

In a flash of inspiration I kicked off my shoes and socks, rolled up my trouser legs to above the knees and waded into the slush. At that moment the bull-killers charged, scattering the heifers, and, seizing the bull by its horns, head, tail and legs, toppled it on to its side. During the next twenty minutes they pounded its huge black belly with their fists, sometimes pausing to ram its snout deep into the dung, and then finally twisting and breaking its neck. And as I photographed the struggle, sometimes standing, sometimes kneeling waist deep in the dung, I had also to keep a vigilant eye on the heifers as they charged this way and that, heads lowered, tails flicking, nostrils snorting. At one stage I slipped and came down on my back, and was covered in dung from neck to toe. Indeed it was little short of a miracle, considering the weight of my cameras, that I was able to keep them clear of the muck.

After the bull had been killed, King Zwelithini, followed by the princes, chiefs and regimental commanders, trudged axe in

Dancing in honour of the new King.

The king and his retinue arrive in the cattlefold for the Bull-Killing ceremony.

hand across the cattlefold to where the carcass lay. An elderly
man named Sombila Mdletshe walked ahead of them carrying
amanzamhlophe, or hallowed 'white water', in a white enamel
basin. Dipping his fingers into the liquid he sprinkled it to left
and right in order to ritually strengthen the king, his regiments
and his subjects. When he reached the slain bull, the king
stepped on to its massive belly, and raising the axe high above
his head struck a *coup de grâce* on the side of its neck. He then
returned to the edge of the cattlefold, and turning around to face

the bull led the warriors in singing an ancient Zulu hymn. About
twenty minutes later he left the cattlefold, followed by his retinue
and the regiments, and returned to his home. I remained behind
to make notes and to photograph the braves who had started
skinning the bull under supervision of the *induna*, Cebekhulu.

When the carcass had been skinned and dismembered it was
hung up along the palisades. Later the portions were hacked
into smaller pieces and cooked, and the choicest parts put aside
for the king to taste. The rest was consumed by the regiments.

Moments before the Bull-Killing ceremony.
The black bull is kept in the centre of a small
herd of cattle.

Regimental commander Cebekhulu who was
in charge of the bull killing.

The bull-killers charge.

The cattle scatter as
the bull is attacked.

198

A cow watches inquisitively as the
bull is being pummelled to death.

The herd nervously crowds together.

The bull-killers being exhorted by frenzied
warriors and spectators.

The young king, axe in hand, stands with his princes, chiefs and regimental commanders beside the carcass of the bull.

King Zwelithini poised to strike the *coup de grâce*.

Right After the bull has been killed the king and his people sing ancient Zulu hymns in the cattlefold.

Below The bull being skinned by menials.

Prince Makhosini Dlamini and Chief Gatsha
Buthelezi after the Bull-Killing ceremony.

Singing praises to Zwelithini KaBhekuzulu,
Lion of the Zulu nation.

Queen Sibongile and
Prince Makhosini
Dlamini at
Khethomthandayo.

At about 3.30 p.m. I left the cattlefold, still caked with drying dung. I accompanied Shange and Mlambo to a hut behind the late King Cyprian's house, where they helped me scrape the gummy mess from my clothes and scrub my legs and feet. In the meantime King Zwelithini had returned to the throne beneath the canopy, and the regiments, having regrouped before him in a semi-circle, could be heard singing and dancing.

A little after four o'clock, looking more like a tramp than a guest of the Zulu royal house, I set out for the scene of activity to take leave of the king and return to Nongoma. I found him in the company of the Swazi prime minister, Makhosini Dlamini, and the other members of the Swazi delegation. Also present was a bevy of Zulu royal women, among them the young queen Sibongile and Buthelezi's mother and sister, the Princesses Magogo and Morjinah. To the immediate right of the throne was a vacant leather armchair, which I learned on greeting the king he had reserved for me. So I sat down beside him suddenly aware that I was the only white man left at Khethomthandayo.

During the hours before sunset we were entertained again to regimental dancing, as well as to a succession of graceful performances by Swazi maidens and various other visiting troupes. Then followed a lengthy recital of Zulu history by the doyen of chroniclers, the illustrious Princess Magogo. Swaggering back and forth in full view of the assembly, a long stave in her hand, she held us spellbound for almost an hour. Even the warriors, feasting on the deluge of words that poured from her talented lips, seemed scarcely to breathe. Foremost of her admirers was Buthelezi himself, who now stood out among the leaders of the regiments. At this stage, my wife and daughters arrived. They had grown concerned at what had become of me, and on enquiry at the gates of Khethomthandayo had been assured by the police that I had emerged unscathed, although immersed in cowdung, from the cattlefold. Brought to the throne by Mlambo, they were welcomed by the king, his queen and Buthelezi.

At sundown the day's proceedings came to an end, and we took leave of King Zwelithini, Buthelezi and the many other members of the Zulu royal house.

Next morning we departed for the Western Cape Province. But my heart remained in Khethomthandayo.

Index